FIRST AID

TW-05

Tactical Wisdom

www.tactical-wisdom.com

COPYRIGHT © 2023 Joseph W Dolio

All Rights Reserved

ISBN-13: 9798862154023

Cover Art: Andrew Dolio

FIRST AID

TACTICAL WISDOM SERIES

TW-05

JOE DOLIO

Copyright 2023. All rights reserved. No part of this publications may be reproduced in any form, or by any means, electronic or mechanical, including photocopying, recording, or any information browsing, storage, or retrieval system, without express permission in writing from the author.

This book contains general information about medical conditions and treatments. The information is not medical advice and should not be treated as such. This first aid manual is not a substitute for hands-on first aid training by an accredited & authorized first aid training provider and must not be used as such.

Neither the author nor anyone else connected to Tactical Wisdom can take any responsibility for the results or consequences of any attempt to use or adopt any of the information presented in this manual.

Pineapple does not belong on pizza.

Nothing in this book should be construed as an attempt to offer or render a medical opinion or otherwise engage in the practice of medicine.

The information contained in this book does not constitute legal advice and should never be relied on as such. Consult with an attorney or other legal professional in your local area.

The information in this book is provided for informational purposes only. Your use of the information in this book is at your own risk.

Epstein did not kill himself.

Bible References are from the NIV, unless otherwise noted.

Preface

*'But I will restore you to health
and heal your wounds,'
declares the Lord…*

Jeremiah 30:17a

What do we envision a Without Rule of Law situation to look like? We don't have to go very far back into history to see it.

The Russo-Ukrainian War and the War in Donbas that led to it give us a prime example in the town of Avdiivka. When the Donetsk People's Republic declared itself a free region in 2014, they captured the town in the middle of April. Ukrainian government forces retook the city in July of 2014, and this pattern has been repeated in Avdiivka ever since.

When Russia invaded Ukraine in 2022, Avdiivka once again found itself on the front lines. Heavy fighting occurred there. Avdiivka has seen nearly daily shelling since 2014.

In 2021, the population was officially estimated at 31,940. As of August 3rd, 2022, the population is estimated at 2,500. More than 90% of the population has fled or died.

In 2017, what has now become known as the First Battle of Avdiivka occurred. The battle raged from January 29, 2017, to February 4, 2017. During this period, the city had no electricity and no heating. It gets cold there. The fighting and cold weather injuries led to enough civilian casualties for UNICEF to declare it a humanitarian disaster.

When a hurricane arrives in a US city, police and fire departments announce that they will stop responding to calls when the wind gets over 40 miles per hour sustained. You will be on your own. Once service resumes, there will not likely be phone service to report your injuries or passable roads for them to get to you.

In the height of the 2020 George Floyd riots, police, fire, and medical responses were almost non-existent. For example, when the self-appointed security forces of the Capitol Hill Autonomous Zone shot several people, police and fire personnel couldn't get to them to treat them or even investigate the assaults.

These are the conditions we envision.

Naming this manual "First Aid" is really a misnomer, because in a true, prolonged WROL situation, we are talking about only-aid. There will be no open emergency room, no ambulances, and probably not even a "Doctor Quinn, Medicine Woman", to help you. You will be on your own.

We need to develop the skills and gather the equipment to be ready to treat any injuries or illnesses, and institute practices that reduce the chance for disease. The time to develop this ability is now.

I've often said that First Aid should be the first preparedness skill you develop because you can use it TODAY. Having some skills and gear with you at all times right now, in normal society can (and does) save lives.

The problem in most preparedness circles is that everyone is focused on conflict. They train to fight with firearms, so they train to treat gunshot wounds, neglecting less "cool" skills like splinting a fracture. I assure you that in a WROL situation, that broken leg can become fatal if you can't get up and move to shelter, food, or water. Diarrhea is an inconvenience today, but it

WILL be fatal in a WROL environment with limited access to clean water to re-hydrate.

I always begin first aid classes with a show of hands, because all anyone wants to talk about is how to treat gunshot wounds. I ask everyone who has ever been in a gunfight to raise their hand (no hands ever go up). Then I ask everyone who has ever fallen down to raise their hand (everyone raises their hand). Based on that alone, shouldn't we focus more time on treating fall injuries?

Another reason to focus on minor injuries (and to avoid cargo shorts) is because without hospitals and readily available anti-biotics, infection becomes a major concern. For everyone's talk of the Rhodesian Light Infantry in their cool-guy Rhodie shorts, they suffered a very large number of non-combat injuries and fatalities due to infection from wading through dirty water with open cuts while wearing their hot shorts.

In a WROL situation, there will be dirt and debris. Unburied bodies lead to pandemics (a pandemic may even be part of the original triggering event). Lack of proper food storage and preparation facilities will lead to foodborne illness, and so on.

We need to learn how to handle these things with absolutely no support.

I frequently point out that self-sufficiency is our goal, because if we are self-sufficient, we cannot be forced to bend the knee to receive what we need. For example, imagine a child getting a compound fracture. You did your best, but beforehand, you focused on gunshot wounds, so you had no idea how to properly set and splint a fracture or keep the wound clean. After a few days, the child has a spiked fever and can't keep food down. There is a FEMA Field Hospital 15 miles away, but to get treatment, the whole family must move inside the camp, unarmed, and they must seize all the extra gear you bring in for "sanitation" reasons. Also, everyone in the camp seems sick, because that many humans living in close quarters in an austere environment ALWAYS leads to illness. Do you want to go into that camp?

Wouldn't self-sufficiency be better?

Let's learn how to be medically self-sufficient.

To appease the lawyers: This book is NOT medical advice and should not be taken as such. In fact, many things will seem to go against current common medical practices. Rely on this book at your own risk.

No book is a substitute for training from a competent instructor. Check with the local Red Cross or Fire Department for first aid training. There are several physical skills here, like bandaging, that MUST be practiced many times before you master it.

Also consider taking a wilderness medicine course.

Get serious about learning and training.

Table of Contents

Tactical Wisdom

First Aid Manual

Chapter 1

WROL First Aid Concepts

Nation will rise against nation, and kingdom against kingdom.
There will be famines and earthquakes in various places.

Matthew 24:7

We live in an instant gratification society. A society where I can order a complex meal and it will arrive in 30-45 minutes as if I had cooked it myself. With a simple phone call, or a few clicks of a mouse I can get anything I want delivered to my door nearly instantly. I can get medical advice in seconds, or in the event of an emergency, an ambulance shows up in minutes. If I don't feel well, I can walk into the hospital and be seen fairly quickly.

But what if that wasn't the case? What if the ambulances weren't coming, the hospital was burned to the ground and my local doctor is dead or has fled the area? The comfortable life in Western nations is the fallacy; the rest of the world already knows these answers: You must take care of it yourself. What if it was a mid-level crisis (COVID) and your hospital told you to go home, and your fire department/ambulance service said they won't risk coming to you? What would you do?

The purpose of this First Aid Manual is to develop very basic first aid skills, acute injury and illness treatment skills, and some basic prevention skills. We're not going to develop you into a US Navy Special Amphibious Reconnaissance Corpsman (SARC), a Special Forces Medic, or an Air Force Pararescue Jumper (PJ). We will borrow some of their skills, but also add some primitive medicine, some wilderness medicine, and some arcane knowledge. We might even dispel an Old Wives Tale or two.

It's important to note that before modern medicine and all its magical treatments and drugs, humans survived and treated injuries for all of human history. Humans have always had people who specialized in caring for and treating the sick and injured. People healed broken bones, cuts, gunshots, and all manner of injuries and illnesses without the wonders of modern medicine.

Like all modern things, we have set aside skills for technology and trinkets that do the work for us, so that we don't have to. We have also outsourced the skill portion to others, so that we don't have to know things.

In this manual, we'll focus on skills. We won't completely eschew modern medicine, because there have been great advancements in modern emergency treatment gear, like tourniquets and hemostatic dressings, that will make injuries more survivable. We will learn how to rely on our skills to take care of ourselves and our friends in an emergency.

Before we go down that route, though, we have to make a couple of agreements on the premise here. First, we are discussing a situation where modern medical treatment at a Trauma Center is not forthcoming or will be severely delayed. This is no "bandage and transport" manual. For the EMTs, Paramedics, Nurses, Doctors, and small men from Louisiana oil rigs who might read this, this isn't what you're used to.

One of the more common issues with first aid manuals, and even military ones, is that they tend to focus on the fact that you will receive advanced care at a medical facility within the first hour of injury, the "Golden Hour". While that may be OK right now, in a WROL situation, there will be no ambulance and going to the Emergency Room might be more dangerous than staying away. There is definitely no Medevac flight inbound.

The second premise we must accept is that these are not skills for the hospital. What I mean is, these skills are the down-and-dirty skills for patching and mending in the field without advanced care and might appear contrary to modern medical advice. Understand that this is not that same medical care as you get in the hospital, and it won't be pretty. Sometimes, the treatments might seem contrary to medical advice, but they are effective. These are the skills to be used when nothing else is available. They are not "book perfect", but rather "good enough".

Let's cover some of the basic guidelines in WROL care.

Basic WROL Medical Guidelines

1. Gloves are your friend. Wearing gloves, even non-medical grade ones, can prevent the transmission of pathogens and will at least keep you safe from contact injuries and biological agents. Wear gloves and have medical grade gloves available.

2. If it's wet and it's not yours, you want to avoid contact with it. Any bodily fluids are dangerous, especially in a situation without advanced antibiotics.

3. Your IFAK (Individual First Aid Kit) is for YOU. Each person in your group must have their own. If someone is unconscious, use their kit on them. This is why you should standardize where everyone carries their IFAK. As an example, certain private military companies require all members of their protective teams to carry the IFAK in their left cargo pocket.

4. Salvage all medical supplies you find. Any time you come across medical supplies in a WROL situation, pick them up even if you have sufficient supplies. You don't know what you will use tomorrow or what kind of an incident you will come across. I'm not saying steal or loot, I'm saying pick up abandoned property.

5. Have "team" kits that are larger. This should be a kit carried by your main medical team for treating more than one person. It's also a supply of extra gear to replace used items.

6. Deal with what caused the injury first, then the injury. If it was a gunfight or assault, win the fight first. If someone was bitten by an aggressive animal, deal with the animal first. If someone was burned, either put out the fire or move them away first. You get the idea.

7. Casualties are expected to self-aid until help is available. If an injured party is conscious, they should tend to their own injuries while the others deal with whatever the situation was. This is especially true with bleeding – getting it under control can't wait.

8. Casualties or injured parties are responsible for self-defense and self-rescue. I can't just give up when I get hurt. If our team was attacked, and I was shot, I still have to defend myself. If I fall in a hole, I can't just wait for someone else to come along.

9. Injured parties may have to remain on their own. If you've fallen in a deep hole, you may have to remain alone and treat your injuries while the team gets a rope set up to come to help you. If your vehicle column was ambushed and the rest of the team was pushed away, you may have to hide, treat your injuries, and defend yourself until they can get back to you.

10. Never attempt a treatment or procedure you haven't practiced. This is vital. You can do more damage than good. In the same vein, don't carry items in your gear that you have no idea how to use (I'm looking at you tacti-cool guys with the 14-gauge needle for tension pneumothorax reduction).

11. Never (ever) be without at least a minimal IFAK. Start TODAY carrying an individual first aid kit. You'll be surprised how often you use it.

12. Replace supplies IMMEDIATELY any time that you use them. If you are away from your supplies, refill them at your first opportunity.

13. Avoid groups of sick people and unburied dead.

14. Never assume water is safe.

15. Don't be afraid to move people. Conventional first aid training says to limit movement until a backboard can be brought in. Most times it's not needed, and delaying movement means risk. Move to a safer location, then treat. This doesn't just apply during combat. Let's say someone was watching your team and saw someone sprain an ankle. While you're all clucking over the twisted ankle, you are distracted and exposed. At least move to cover first.

16. Establish 360-degree security before beginning treatment.

Treating Strangers

Treating strangers you come across is a risky proposition, but the lesson of the Good Samaritan tells us that we should still do it whenever we can. We're going to discuss how we can do that, while minimizing our risk.

Understand first that the "injured person" has been a set-up for ambush and robbery since man's earliest days. Know the risk and only offer help if you can do so securely. Place some team members in concealed over-watch positions before advancing to help, and even then, bring along another person for in-close security.

Before asking how you can help, ask the person if there is any danger in the immediate area. Maybe they got bit by a snake or maybe a Chinese ambush team or band of thugs is holding their kids hostage, so always ask first. Ask the injured party exactly what happened to them. In Iraq, the insurgents attached bombs to 3rd parties while holding their family hostage and forced them to commit attacks, so ask the question.

Ask the injured person where their first aid kit is and use their kit before using any of your supplies. This is important – never put your IFAK and therefore your life at risk by using it on others in a dangerous environment. The same holds true with water. Help them get access to their own water, but don't compromise your own limited supply.

Provide whatever treatment you can, and then LEAVE. Do not get into the habit of bringing home strays, no matter what their story is. There are always exceptions, but don't invite others inside your perimeter. Explain that you have helped all that you can and that you have to move on.

Finally, don't be afraid to just keep going. You can't save everyone, nor is it your responsibility. We should certainly help whenever it is feasible to do so, but not if doing so requires us to take on unacceptable risk. If there are security issues in the area or you are already trying to break contact with a hostile group, you can't stop. If there is a place where obviously there is a rampant illness in a large group of people, the right thing to do is to avoid that area, no matter how much it tugs at our heartstrings. They're already sick, you are not.

Treatment of Hostile Parties

Yes, we sometimes will have to treat hostile parties. In the current situation, treating someone after a self-defense incident can go a long way towards showing who the good guy was in court.

One of the biggest dangers we have in a WROL situation is the loss of our morality. It's easy to see those would harm us or steal from us as somehow less than us, but we must not sink to their level. Make no mistake, one who attacks others deserves whatever happens to them, but what separates us from them is our mercy. Mercy is unearned, we give it regardless, when it is feasible to do so.

But, under what conditions do we offer treatment to those who fought us a few moments ago? How can we do so safely and securely?

First, before offering or attempting treatment, the subject must no longer be a threat. Those wounded, even gravely, can still pose a deadly threat.

We only treat hostile parties when:

1. They have clearly and unequivocally surrendered.

2. They are completely disarmed and searched.

3. They are removed from reach of any weapons.

Consider handcuffing, flex-cuffing, or securing the hands in some other way if possible. Use their first aid supplies, before expending any of your own.

8

Also, have another member of your team maintain a security overwatch from outside of arms reach.

Storage of Medical Supplies

At your home location, whatever that is, medical gear should be a tightly protected supply. I can get more food, but probably not more medical gear. Store your excess medical gear in a secure fashion to ensure that you have it when you need it.

Limit access to the medical supply storage to your medical team and your leadership team. This ensures that the gear is accounted for.

Store it in a cool, dry place, protected from the elements. A lot of medical equipment loses its efficacy when exposed to temperature extremes or dampness.

Keep medical supplies organized so that you can find what you need quickly. Organization also helps you know what you need should an opportunity to barter come up or if a team is being sent out to scavenge for gear. Storing them in portable containers like duffel bags or ammo cans is a good idea. Avoid backpacks, because everyone will probably already be carrying a backpack. You can carry a backpack and a duffel bag at the same time.

Notes from the USAF Pararescue Jumpers

- For care under fire, the priority is:

    o SHOOT BACK.

    o TOURNIQUET.

        o   MOVE THE CASUALTY.

- After the fight:

        o   Stop the bleeding.

        o   Get them breathing.

        o   Get them ready to leave.

These tips will get you and your combat casualties out of the area the fastest. After getting away from the site of the contact, then you can apply better care.

Conclusion

These guidelines should be able to serve as a basic SOP (Standard Operating Procedure) for your medical operations. If we start from the same assumptions and follow basic guidelines we can safely and effectively treat injuries and illnesses that occur, even if it's not to modern medical standards.

Remember, we are not treating to hold someone over until they get to a hospital; we are providing field treatment and care in an austere environment with no hope of advanced medical care.

Training Standard

1. List at least 5 basic WROL medical guidelines.

2. Describe the guidelines for providing treatment to strangers.

3. Describe the guidelines for providing treatment to hostile parties.

4. Explain methods for the storing and organization of medical gear.

5. List the priorities of care under fire.

Tactical Wisdom

First Aid Manual

Chapter 2

Medical Kits

He went to him and bandaged his wounds, pouring on oil and wine. Then he put the man on his own donkey, brought him to an inn and took care of him.

Luke 10:34

In the tale of the Good Samaritan, everyone else avoided the wounded man and walked around him, until the Samaritan showed up, with the proper gear, and treated the man's injuries, and got him to better care. The Good Samaritan didn't just have the heart to help, he had the proper supplies and skills at hand. That's the lesson for us.

This biggest issue I have with our current world situation is that every time we have a mass shooting or vehicle attack, everyone stands around filming and those who do try to render aid do so with no proper gear. We live in a time when there is literally no excuse not to always have at least a compact kit with you with a tourniquet, some hemostatic gauze, and a pressure bandage.

In fact, with everyone carrying backpacks and large purses, there is no reason to have an advanced IFAK (Individual First Aid Kit) on your person. In this chapter, we will discuss how to build various kits to be carried with you or in your vehicle.

While our focus is on WROL first aid, these kits can, and should, be built and carried on a daily basis right now. Don't get complacent, carry some type of kit with you everywhere you go. You never know when a car accident, fall, or more severe incident like a shooting will occur. Be ready at all times.

Reminder: Never put an item in ANY of your kits that you do not know how to use. You must be well versed in any item you carry. Not just "seen it done once" but trained and done enough repetitions to be effective. Lives are on the line, so train.

Bleed Kit

A bleed kit is a smaller first aid kit for dealing with massive bleeding or severe trauma. Exsanguination (bleeding out) is the biggest immediate danger in traumatic injuries, so it must be dealt with first.

In situations where carrying a full kit isn't practical, a bleed kit can fill the gap. For example, in an office setting, you could carry a bleed kit in a pocket, and your full kit in your backpack or purse. Tactically, you could carry a bleed kit on your chest rig or war belt, and your full kit can be attached to your backpack. It's an immediate need kit.

The bleed kit can also be part of your full first aid kit, but in a separate bag or pouch designed to be pulled out with one hand quickly.

Bleed Kit Contents:

- Tourniquet (CAT or SWAT-T preferably)
    - Note: Pre-stage the TQ by taking it out of the plastic and feeding the strap through the gate. You need to be able to put it on under stress and one handed with either hand.

- Hemostatic Gauze (Cellox/QuikClot type)

- Pressure Bandage

- 4-Inch Gauze Pad

- Chest Seals – 2

- Mini Permanent Marker (for writing the time on the TQ)

- Nitrile gloves

- Trauma shears

This might seem like a big list, but placed in the right container, it compresses down pretty small. This should be carried at all times. I also toss in a mini notebook to make notes on, like time things were applied, time bleeding stopped, etc. These notes can help whoever provides follow-on treatment, even if it's you yourself who does the follow-on.

In the current world situation, the American Council of Surgeons recommends that everyone have a bleed kit immediately available. It's really that important.

Individual First Aid Kit (IFAK)

These are called many things by many people, like the "Personal Trauma Kit" or "Blowout Kit", but we're going to go with the industry standard Individual First Aid Kit, because it's a first aid kit designed for an individual, YOU.

That's our first point on the IFAK. While you CAN use your IFAK to treat others now, in a WROL situation, you should NEVER use your IFAK on anybody but you. The reason I say this is because right now, I can use the kit to save a life, and when I get home, I can restock it. In a WROL situation, if I use my IFAK on someone on day 1 of a 3-day scouting mission, I'm at risk for the next 2 days.

My solution to this is that I carry my personal IFAK in the butt pack of my war belt (I know, all you cool guys don't wear butt packs or carry canteens – that's because you're going home at the end of the day during training). I carry a second IFAK attached to my backpack that I can treat others with. This way, I don't deplete my own IFAK. I also carry an extra pressure dressing inside my pack, because one may need to be changed.

The contents can be modified, but the items on the list presented here are the bare minimum requirements. In other words, you may add to this list, and we'll give some ideas, but you should have every item on this list at a minimum.

Remember also person specific needs. For example, if someone is asthmatic, include a rescue inhaler. Tailor your IFAK to YOU. A team medic should carry extras of these items, if you have extra, as well.

IFAK Minimum Contents:

- CAT or SWAT-Tourniquet (avoid RATS Tourniquet)

- Trauma Pressure Bandages

- Trauma Pads/ABD Pads

- Chest Seals or Occlusive Dressings (at least 2)

- Rolled Gauze

- Gauze Pads (4x4 & 3x3)

- Clotting Agent/Gauze (Quik-Clot/Cellox)

- Medical Tape

- Duct Tape

- Nasopharyngeal or Oropharyngeal Airway (with lube)

- CPR Barrier

- Gloves (Nitrile is better)

- Triangular Bandage (preferably green or black)

- Self-Conforming Bandage (ACE-type, not brightly colored) and SAM Splint

- Triple Anti-Biotic (either wipes or tube)

• EMT Shears

• Casualty Blanket/Space Blanket (small, lightweight type)

These are the BARE MINIMUM.

Some of the things I like to add are:

> • Small Light – You can never have too many.
>
> • Tweezers
>
> • Small spray bottle of hydrogen peroxide for cleaning
>
> • Hemostats/clamps – Many uses
>
> • Anti-Septic wipes
>
> • Eye wash/eye pads

Other items beyond these belong in larger team kits.

Vehicle First Aid Kit

In addition to each person always having their own IFAK on them, each vehicle should contain a larger Vehicle First Aid Kit. This would hold more of the same items that are in your IFAK, plus some more advanced items.

> • Tourniquets – At least 2 extra.
>
> • Pressure bandages – 2-4

- Various gauze pads – A good supply of gauze pads in various sizes (2x2, 3x3, 4x4, and ABD pads).

- Extra chest seals - At least 2.

- Several rolls of gauze in various widths.

- QuikClot/Hemostatic gauze

- Medical tape – At least 4 rolls.

- Gloves – Keep a box in the kit.

- Airways – various sizes (learn how to use them).

- Several triangular bandages/rolled bandages.

- SAM splints – at least 2. Consider various sizes.

- Heavy duty casualty blanket – One that is substantial enough that you could drag somebody on it.

- Burn dressings.

- Hydrocortisone cream/antibiotic cream.

- Epi-Pen and antihistamine.

- Saline/hydrogen peroxide.

- Various pain/inflammation medications (aspirin, ibuprofen, etc.).

- Ice packs.

- Hand sanitizer/disinfectant wipes.

Team Aid Kit

Your team's dedicated medic should carry a slightly larger kit, in addition to their own IFAK, for treating the team. This kit can also be used, rather than IFAKs, to treat third parties you come across in need of treatment but remember that supplies used on others are gone forever.

Normally, this kit should be packed in a pouch on the outside of the medic's ruck or backpack. That way, everyone can find it and use it should the medic be occupied by treating someone else or injured themselves. This kit should also be clearly marked with the international first aid symbol. It doesn't have to be a big red on white patch, but at least a black on green or green on black cross. This way, under stress, it can be found and understood as a first aid kit immediately, without digging through it.

Most of the items in it are the same as the items in your IFAKs, just in greater quantity. It can be used to restock IFAKs in the field if needed.

Team Aid Kit Contents:

- 5 Pairs Nitrile Gloves

- 2 Nasopharyngeal Airways (with lubricant)

- Petrolatum Gauze – For dressing burns.

- 1 set Chest Seals

- 2 Tourniquets

- 4 - 6 in. Emergency Trauma Dressings

- 4 Rolls Gauze

- 2 Rolls Self-Conforming Bandages

- Abdominal Emergency Trauma Dressings (2-4)

- 2 Hemostatic Dressings (QuikClot/other)

- 2 SAM Splints

- Trauma Shears

- 2 Rolls Medical Tape

- Electrolyte packets – can be added to water to rehydrate people.

- Glucose gels

In addition, if your medic knows how to use them, they should carry 2 14-gauge decompression needle kits. Notice that the only place this belongs is in the Team Aid Kit, not in every person's gear. These should be the kind in their own hard case that is sealed for safety.

Another addition, if your medic is properly trained, are saline lock kits and rubber bands for setting up IV's. You could then also stock whatever IV fluids that your medic knows how to administer.

These are vital supplies, and the medic should guard them. No one should be taking things out of the Team Aid Kit without the medic's approval. Remember, you're more likely to get hurt falling down than in a gunfight, so keep the supplies where they belong.

Medications

In the Baseline Training Manual (TW-01), we gave a list of OTC medications that your team should stockpile. We're going to repeat that list here and add a few others.

In addition to these medications, any prescription medications that any member of your team needs should be added. In the event of a total collapse or grid-down situation, your team should also be picking up any clearly labeled medication they come across that your medical group knows how to administer. These can be stored until needed.

Remember, expiration dates are not always absolute. In the world of medicine, medication might lose some of its efficacy, but most are still good for years beyond the expiration date. This is not medical advice, make your own decisions upon consulting with your own medical team.

Reminder: No one should be allowed to remain armed if they are taking any medication that affects their judgment, their ability to operate machinery, or causes drowsiness.

Stock as many cough drops as possible. Anyone manning an observation post or conducting patrols should carry them to quiet coughs. Cough syrup can help as well but be aware of what else is in the cough syrup that may affect reaction times or judgment.

OTC Medication List:

- Hand Sanitizer: At least 60% alcohol

- Ibuprofen: Motrin/Advil

- Naproxen: Aleve - Longer lasting pain relief.

- Aspirin: In addition to pain relief, it is a blood thinner.

- Acetaminophen: (Tylenol) You can alternate Ibuprofen and Acetaminophen every 2 hours if needed.

- Diphenhydramine: (Benadryl) In addition to its life-saving antihistamine properties, Benadryl can be used as a sleep aid or calming agent.

- Loperamide: (Imodium) - Anti-Diarrheal medication can save your life in a WROL situation as diarrhea causes dehydration.

- Laxatives: Constipation kills people. Yes, really.

- Pseudoephedrine: (Sudafed) - An excellent decongestant, but stockpiling it has been made difficult as it's so tightly controlled, despite being OTC.

- Fexofenadine HCl: (Allegra) - another antihistamine for allergies.

- Meclizine: (Dramamine) - This is a motion sickness treatment, which can be used to treat nausea/vomiting. It also helps with anxiety.

- Hydrocortisone: For wound treatment

- Bacitracin: For wound treatment

- Orajel/Cankaid: For mouth pain or sores.

- Loratadine: (Claritin/Alavert) For treatment of allergy symptoms like runny nose, itchy eyes, sneezing.

- Lotrimin: Treats fungal infections in various places.

- Cold medicine: Anything containing dextromethorphan and guaifenesin.

- Ranitidine: (Zantac) For treatment of heartburn and ulcers.

Additionally, keeping a rescue inhaler or two on hand can help when someone is experiencing respiratory distress. As with anything else, if someone has asthma on your team, stock their regular asthma medication, as rescue inhalers are not a replacement for it.

Conclusion

Having first aid kits is something you can do right now. It's the one preparedness thing that applies to your life right now. No matter what you are preparing for, medical situations or injuries will occur.

Commit right now to building at least an IFAK or Bleed Kit immediately (before you go any farther in this book) and to carrying it EVERY SINGLE DAY. Yes, it's tedious. Yes, it's extra weight. It is also far better than bleeding out on the side of the road.

Training Standard

1. Explain why you should carry a kit every single day.

2. Build a Bleed Kit.

3. Build an IFAK.

4. Build a Vehicle First Aid Kit.

5. Build a Team Aid Kit.

6. List at least 10 OTC medications to keep on hand.

Tactical Wisdom

First Aid Manual

Chapter 3

Initial Assessment

*From the sole of your foot to the top of your head
there is no soundness—
only wounds and welts and open sores,
not cleansed or bandaged or soothed with olive oil.*

Isaiah 1:6

The first step in treating any kind of injury is to find out what the problem is, or the problems are. When we see something happen, it's easy to know what's wrong. With a conscious patient, we can usually just ask what is wrong. However, sometimes someone doesn't know what happened, is disoriented, or may be unconscious.

What we need is a system to help us evaluate someone to figure out what needs to be done. That's where Initial Assessment comes into play.

But before we can even treat someone, we have to assess the safety of the scene. If we rush out into the open to check on a down person, and they were shot by a sniper, what do you think is going to happen to you? If we quickly turn them over and they were laying on a live wire, you are now a casualty. They could be laying very still because they are on an unstable surface and you rushing out there can plunge you both down into a basement.

Scene Safety Assessment

In a WROL environment, there will be more bad actors active than in the current scenario, so security must be our first concern. Take steps to secure the area before attempting to treat any injured party. If a fight of some type is what led to the injuries, win the fight and then secure the local area first, with personnel watching in each direction. If you just happen across a downed person and decide to help them, post sentries first and make sure the area is secure before moving on.

Even in the current situation, pause and assess the scene before approaching any injured party. Look to see who is standing around and assess what might have been the mechanics of injury. For example, if they appear to have been struck by falling debris, look up and see if you will be in danger as well. If they appear to have fallen through a floor, assess the ability of that floor to hold you as you approach them.

Always assess scene safety first, because you becoming a casualty as well means that no one gets aid.

Note: Post-WROL, I recommend wearing any type of mask when treating people you don't know. Disease will be a problem and even wrapping a shemagh or lifting a neck gaiter over your mouth and nose will provide some level of protection. Gloves are REQUIRED.

Also, post-WROL, ALWAYS establish security in a 360 degree perimeter before anyone attempts to provide care. Your focus will be on providing care, someone else must provide security.

Even when the power is out, be aware of downed power lines. A current applied to the wire anywhere along it will send the current down the line. It's better to be safe than sorry.

Initial Assessment – MARCH

When dealing with an injured person or an unconscious person, we can apply what is known as the MARCH Algorithm to determine what needs to be done. It's a memory aid to ensure that we check for all the major causes of death in trauma cases. We apply the MARCH Algorithm first, then move on to other steps.

M	Massive hemorrhage/bleeding control
A	Airway management
R	Respiratory management
C	Circulation/shock management
H	Head injury/hypothermia

Massive Hemorrhage

The first and most immediate concern is called exsanguination, or bleeding to death. The body holds a finite amount of blood and massive hemorrhage will quickly drain that to a level below what is required to sustain life.

Check the victim (or yourself) immediately for any bleeding. Start at the head and work your way down, looking for evidence of massive hemorrhage, like flowing blood or spurting blood. During the MARCH phase, we are NOT worried about minor cuts and scrapes, we are talking about major bleeding.

If major bleeding is found, apply a tourniquet directly to the skin 2-3 inches above the injury. In a combat or unsecure situation, the casualty should self-apply a tourniquet high and tight on the extremity where the wound is (as close to the armpit or groin as possible). It can be converted to a tourniquet closer to the injury later, the key is to try to stop the massive hemorrhage as soon as possible.

When applying a tourniquet, use the "MF'r" rule. Yes, that MF. The tourniquet is not tight enough unless the patient shouts an obscenity. While it's a fun way to remember this, it's vital. Most tourniquets are not applied tight enough to slow down or stop circulation. Wrench it down another half turn after the obscenity.

NOTE: Never apply a tourniquet over a joint. Do it above or below the joint.

Write the time on the tourniquet using a permanent marker. If the patient is unconscious, write a large "T" on their forehead, so that anyone else treating them will know a tourniquet has been applied.

If the first tourniquet did not stop the building in short order, apply a second one. The second one should be applied side by side with the first.

Never leave a tourniquet on for more than 2 hours, or permanent damage may result.

The two biggest errors are waiting too long to apply a tourniquet and not applying it tight enough.

If you don't have a commercial tourniquet (you should), you can improvise one with a triangular bandage folded into a flat strip or with a belt. Wrap it around the limb and tie a square knot on it. Place a stick or rod through the knot and start tightening. Once the flow has stopped or slowed significantly, tie the stick or rod in place.

Once the bleeding has stopped or slowed significantly, convert the tourniquet by applying a pressure bandage to the wound and removing the tourniquet. Hemostatic agents can help here too. I know nurses and doctors will tell you to never remove a tourniquet and let them do it, but we're talking about a situation where there will be no emergency room staff to convert it. Go ahead. It has to be done to prevent permanent damage.

Airway Management

Check to make sure that the patient's airway is open. If they are conscious, ask them if they can breathe. If they can't, or are unconscious, use the head tilt-jaw lift technique to open the airway by moving the tongue.

Head Tilt-Jaw Lift Technique

- Kneel at the level of the casualty's shoulders.
- Place one hand on the casualty's forehead and apply firm, backward pressure with the palm to tilt the head back.
- Place the fingertips of the other hand under the bony part of the lower jaw and lift, bringing the chin forward.

31

- Do not use the thumb to lift.
- Do not completely close the casualty's mouth.
- Do not press deeply into the soft tissue under the chin with the fingers.

Conscious patients can be told to sit or lie in whatever position makes breathing the easiest. Unconscious patients should be placed in the recovery position.

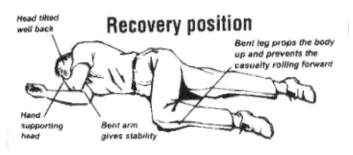

Recovery position

Head tilted well back

Bent leg props the body up and prevents the casualty rolling forward

Hand supporting head

Bent arm gives stability

If the patient is unconscious, insert a nasopharyngeal airway (NPA), through the nasal opening. Remember to lubricate it first. Never insert a nasopharyngeal airway on a conscious patient, it tends not to go very well.

The NPA should go in easily. If you meet resistance, try the other nostril.

Respiratory Management

Next, observe the chest to see if they are breathing. You should be able to see the chest or belly rise and fall. You can also tilt your head and listen for breathing with your ear and feel for exhalation on your cheek.

If they are not breathing, immediately re-check the airway and administer two "rescue breaths". Rescue breaths involve pinching the nose closed and sealing your mouth over theirs. Use a CPR shield/mask if available. Give two long breaths of about one second each, with five to six seconds between. Watch to see if the chest rises and falls.

After attempting two rescue breaths, if breathing isn't restored, skip down to Circulation in the algorithm.

If they are breathing, but it's labored or difficult, check for chest injuries.

The first one to check for is a sucking chest wound. Any open wound to the chest cavity should immediately have an occlusive dressing or chest seal (they're the same thing) placed on it immediately, directly over the wound. The dressings have instructions on them.

If you just have a pressure dressing, you can make do by using the wrapper to make a seal. Place the sterile side of the wrapper down on the wound and cover with the pressure dressing. Use medical tape to secure three sides of the improvised dressing, leaving side closest to the ground open to vent the wound. Have the victim lay on the wound to help seal it.

If the chest seal isn't a vented kind (marked on the package), you may occasionally have to "burp" the dressing. If the patient returns to labored breathing, lift one corner of the bandage for a few seconds to let out trapped air, then reseal.

Any time there is an entrance wound to the chest, check for an exit wound on the opposite side. For this reason, never buy single chest seals – buy them in two packs.

If the victim had major chest trauma and there is no open wound, they may have tension pneumothorax (collapsed lung). Someone on your team should be trained in using a 14-gauge needle to decompress the lung, but it will not be included in this manual. I am intentionally leaving it out to encourage you to go and get real-world physical training.

Circulation

In this segment we are checking to make sure that blood is flowing as it should. Check for a pulse. The best place to check is the carotid artery. Always use your first two fingers to check.

If there is no pulse, immediately begin CPR (See CPR/AED Use Chapter).

Check for and dress any secondary wounds to ensure adequate blood volume.

If the first tourniquet was applied over clothing, apply a new one directly to the skin and remove the first one.

Assess any tourniquets applied to see if the bleeding has stopped. If it has, apply a dressing to the wound and remove the tourniquet, noting the time that you removed it. Continue to monitor for renewed bleeding.

Tourniquets should always be converted to dressings in under 2 hours if possible.

Head Injuries/Hypothermia

Assess the patient's mental state. Anyone in an altered mental state should be disarmed immediately (including knives).

Ask questions to see if they are aware of their surroundings and fully aware. Checking the pupils with a light can tell whether they have a head injury (concussion), as the pupils may not be of equal size and may not dilate or react when a light is shined in them.

Watch for shock. A shock victim may be restless, thirsty, and possibly may sweat despite cool skin. The skin, especially around the mouth, may turn blue (cyanotic).

Make the patient comfortable, loosen their clothing, and reassure them. Cover them with a casualty blanket to keep them warm. Pay close attention to them.

Secondary Assessment

After completing MARCH, we move on to a secondary assessment for a complete check for injuries.

The guide for the secondary assessment is PAWS.

P	Pain and pain management
A	Antibiotics
W	Wounds
S	Splinting

We begin by asking the patient where it hurts and addressing those areas. Conduct a head-to-toe sweep by hand, asking the patient to tell you when it hurts. Lightly squeeze as you move down the arms and legs, and press gently on the torso. Look at your hands after sweeping each section to look for blood from previously unknown injuries.

If the patient is in a lot of pain and you have pain medications, administer them (Tylenol and Ibuprofen types before moving on to anything stronger – pharmacology is beyond the scope of this book). Yes, I am giving the standard Fleet Medical Corpsman advice of "Ibuprofen, a full canteen of water, and change your socks".

If there are breaks in the skin, apply antibiotic lotions to them. If you have "other" antibiotics (prescription), administer them during this phase. Infection is a killer and will be even more so in a WROL situation, so be liberal with antibiotics.

Next, dress all wounds, from little boo-boos to large cuts. Clean them out, apply antibiotics, and cover them. Keeping dirt and contamination out early is how you prevent infection.

Finally, splint any fractures. We will discuss splinting in a later chapter, but splinting is the final phase in trauma treatment.

SAMPLE

If you come across a conscious person having a medical emergency and you need to quickly assess them without the need for the full trauma protocols above, you can use the acronym SAMPLE. This is good, for example, in a current world situation when find someone obviously ill or in distress.

- S: Signs and Symptoms – Signs are what you can observe, and symptoms are what the victim tells you or describes. Use questions to delve deeper. For example, if they report pain, ask them if it's a dull pain, shooting pain, or throbbing pain, etc.
- A: Allergies – Determine if they are allergic to anything in the environment or any medications.

- M: Medication – Ask them what medications they are taking that could have caused a reaction or medications that they should have taken and didn't.
- P: Pertinent Medical History – as simple as "has this ever happened before or anything similar?". Ask about other medical conditions as well.
- L: Last Food/Drink – This could give clues as to allergic reactions or explain fainting/weakness. It's a good idea to also ask them when they last slept.
- E: Events Leading Up To – Ask them what they were doing just before they felt ill or got injured.

Recap

First and foremost, remember that there is no medical treatment while a fight is still going on. Casualties will be expected to self-treat, get themselves to cover, and defend themselves if necessary until after the fight is over.

In an accident, scene safety comes before treatment. Check to make sure you won't also become a patient before rushing to help.

We use the MARCH and PAWS acronyms to help us remember how to treat traumatic injuries and not miss a step.

Training Standard

1. Discuss what is meant by scene safety and how you can assure it.

2. Describe the personal protection steps you can take while treating others.

3. Recite the MARCH algorithm.

4. Demonstrate the proper application of a tourniquet.

5. Describe when to convert a tourniquet to dressing.

6. Demonstrate the head tilt/chin lift technique.

7. Demonstrate placing someone in the recovery position.

8. Recite the PAWS acronym and what steps should be taken during each step.

9. Recite and describe the SAMPLE acronym.

Tactical Wisdom

First Aid Manual

Chapter 4

CPR/AED Use

Then the Lord God formed a man from the dust of the ground and breathed into his nostrils the breath of life, and the man became a living being.

Genesis 2:7

When the heart is stopped, and there is no breathing, a person is dead. CPR and rescue breathing can save a life, however. It's a vital skill that everyone needs to know.

First, while we're going to fully describe the process, I *HIGHLY* recommend taking a CPR/AED course. They occur frequently and are low cost. What is the power to preserve a life worth to you?

Second, a lot of people are fearful of doing CPR because they are afraid of harming the victim. Let's be real here, they are already dead. You can't possibly hurt them. If you break a couple of ribs, but they start breathing and pumping blood again, you're still on the plus side, because THEY WERE DEAD.

As far as fear of civil liability, every state has a law that protects you if you are in good faith trying to save a life. Never let fear of liability stop you. Imagine how they are going to sound to a jury during that lawsuit: "You see, I was dead, and this dude came up and saved my life. But he broke my rib." Don't sweat it. Human life is precious.

Let's talk though about the reality of care in a Without Rule of Law situation or in a wilderness/back country rescue. The reality is that without access to modern medical care in less than 40 minutes, CPR is most likely a losing proposition. It is highly unlikely to work and may put your team at an unacceptable risk level for a technique that is likely to fail. Make good decisions.

Rescue Breathing

I know we covered it before, but let's talk about it again.

All mammals need oxygen to survive. We get that through breathing. We breathe in oxygen from the air, in our lungs the oxygen gets transferred to the blood and waste gases like carbon dioxide get breathed out through exhalation.

If someone is not breathing, first we use the chin tilt-jaw lift method to clear the airway:

Head Tilt-Jaw Lift Technique

- Kneel at the level of the casualty's shoulders.
- Place one hand on the casualty's forehead and apply firm, backward pressure with the palm to tilt the head back.

- Place the fingertips of the other hand under the bony part of the lower jaw and lift, bringing the chin forward.
- Do not use the thumb to lift.
- Do not completely close the casualty's mouth.
- Do not press deeply into the soft tissue under the chin with the fingers.

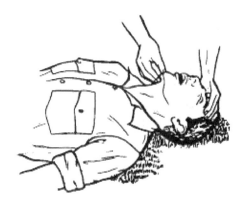

If this doesn't restore breathing, immediately begin rescue breathing:

- Maintain the head tilt-jaw lift method while pinching the nostrils closed using the thumb and index fingers of your hand on the casualty's forehead.
- Take a regular breath and make an airtight seal around the casualty's mouth with your mouth.
- Give one slow breath (lasting one second) into the casualty's mouth, watching for the chest to rise and

fall and listening and feeling for air to escape upon your cheek.
- If the chest rises and air escapes give a second slow breath. If not, reposition the airway.

You can also use your gloved fingers to sweep the mouth, to remove any obstructions.

If there is no pulse and no breathing after two full rescue breaths, move immediately into CPR.

Remember, you can't hurt them; the worst that can happen is that they STAY DEAD. Unless there are obvious reasons not to, like devastating and irreparable trauma (decapitation, etc.), it is ALWAYS worth it to try and save a life by performing CPR – if it safe to do so.

CPR

Let me begin by saying that the American Heart Association dropped rescue breathing from their guidelines for CPR, preferring to have untrained people focus on just giving chest compressions until an ambulance arrives. We don't have that luxury. No ambulances are coming.

Our guidelines will be 30 chest compressions followed by two rescue breaths. While we have already described rescue breathing above, we will give the full procedure here.

- Check for signs of circulation as follows:
  - o Attempt to feel the casualty's carotid pulse (do not take more than 10 seconds).

- While maintaining the airway, place the index and middle fingers of your hand on the casualty's throat.
- Slide the fingers into the groove beside the casualty's Adam's apple and feel for a pulse for no longer than 10 seconds.

○ If the casualty has a carotid pulse but is not breathing, perform rescue breathing.
- Maintain the chin-lift method while pinching the nostrils closed using the thumb and index fingers of your hand that is on the casualty's forehead.
- Take a regular breath and make an airtight seal around the casualty's mouth with your mouth.
- Give one slow breath (lasting one second) into the casualty's mouth, watching for the chest to rise and fall and listening and feeling for air to escape upon your cheek.
- If the chest rises and air escapes give a second slow breath. If not, reposition the airway.

○ If you do not definitely feel a pulse within 10 seconds, perform 5 cycles of compressions and breaths (30 compressions to 2 breaths) starting with compressions (compressions-airway-breathing sequence).

○ Chest Compression Procedure:
- Ensure that the casualty is positioned on a hard, flat surface, in a supine position. Kneel next to the casualty.

- Position yourself on the casualty's side.
- Place the heel of one hand on the center of the casualty's chest on the lower half of the breastbone.
- Place the heel of your other hand on top of the first hand.
- Straighten your arms and lock your elbows and position your shoulders directly over your hands.
- Give 30 compressions.
- Push hard and fast.
- Press down at least 2 inches (5 centimeters) with each compression.
  - After 30 compressions, give two full rescue breaths.
  - Repeat.
  - If a pulse is present, continue rescue breathing at the following rate:
    - Adults: 12 to 20 breaths per minute.
    - Children (one year of age to onset of puberty): 15 to 30 breaths per minute.
    - Infants (less than one year of age): 25 to 50 breaths per minute.

After 5 cycles, you will likely be exhausted. With two rescuers, you should switch off every 5 cycles in order to continue CPR as long as possible. There are stories of people being revived after very long CPR sessions so it's worth it if you can continue.

If you just can't go on due to exhaustion, remember, you didn't let them die, they were already dead. You tried to prolong life.

<u>Automated External Defibrillator Use</u>

The Automated External Defibrillator, or AED as it is commonly known, is a battery-operated machine designed to monitor the heart and administer a shock to the heart if needed to restart it or correct an arrythmia.

Once a WROL situation begins, if you don't already have one, salvage an AED from a looted or abandoned building. They are in all buildings open to the public. It's not a bad idea to quickly secure one if your group doesn't already have one.

The system is designed to be used by untrained people and it will walk you through the steps.

- Turn on the AED. Most turn on automatically when you open the lid, but others may have a button.
- Make sure that the victim is not lying in water.
- Follow the voice prompts.
    - ○ The prompts will direct you to place the pads on the victim.
    - ○ The pads describe where you should put them.
- Everyone should step back - no one should be touching the victim while the AED analyzes the heart rhythm.
- The AED will advise you to either begin chest compressions or to press the shock button.
- Before pressing the button, again make sure no one is touching the victim.
- Press the SHOCK button when prompted.
- The AED will again analyze the heart and will then give further instructions.

Training Standard

1. Demonstrate the head tilt-jaw lift technique.

2. Describe rescue breathing.

3. Describe the steps involved in CPR.

4. Explain the number of cycles to perform of 30 compressions to 2 breaths before checking for a pulse.

5. Explain how to use an Automated External Defibrillator.

Tactical Wisdom

First Aid Manual

Chapter 5

Choking

···but the worries of this life, the deceitfulness of wealth and the desires for other things come in and choke the word, making it unfruitful.

Mark 4:19

Choking is a serious risk. It's a leading cause of death, especially in children under 5. Time is of the essence when dealing with choking. Again, in a WROL situation, we cannot just call 911 and hope for the best. Even in a fully functioning society, a choking incident requires YOUR intervention immediately to prevent a much worse medical situation.

Choking happens when something blocks the airway. Most commonly, it's partially chewed food or some swallowed foreign object, but in trauma care it can also be blood or other body fluids, or even tracheal swelling (one of my favorite Tang Soo Do moves is a web-of-hand strike to the throat).

Recognizing choking is fairly easy. Difficulty breathing, a high-pitched wheeze, and an inability to speak are usually the first signs. Panic quickly sets in and you may see blue (cyanotic) lips.

The universal sign for choking is hardwired into all of us and is instantly recognizable:

Universal Choking Sign

Source: US Army

Understand that if full breathing is not restored, brain cells will begin dying rapidly. Time is of the essence.

If a person can cough, let them cough and try to dislodge the obstruction themselves.

Ask the person if they can breathe. If they cannot breathe, and cannot cough, it's time to intervene. Explain what you are doing and that you are helping first.

Begin with back blows to try and help them dislodge the object.

To administer back blows:

1. Have the victim bend over as parallel to the ground as they can.

2. Brace them diagonally with one hand under the near armpit and supporting the opposite shoulder.
3. Give five sharp blows to the victim's back with the heel of your hand directly between the shoulder blades.

If this doesn't dislodge the object, immediately move to abdominal thrusts.

1. Stand the person and step behind them, placing your lead foot between their feet.
2. Reach around the victim with your weak hand and use two fingers to locate their navel.
3. Place the thumb side of your strong hand fist above your two fingers.
4. Wrap your support hand around the fist.
5. Pull sharply inward and upward five times to dislodge the item.

If this is unsuccessful, lay them down and use your fingers to sweep their mouth to try and dislodge any blockage.

If the victim becomes unresponsive, immediately move to rescue breathing and CPR if needed.

If the victim was unconscious and you suspect choking based on what everyone saw or you saw as you approached, you can deliver abdominal thrusts on them while they are laying on the ground.

1. Kneel astride the victim (near their thighs).
2. Place the heel of one hand against the victim's abdomen (slightly above the navel but below the breastbone). Place your other hand on top of the first one. Point your fingers toward the casualty's head.
3. Press into the casualty's abdomen with a quick, forward and upward thrust 6 to 10 times. Use your body weight to perform the maneuver. Deliver each thrust quickly and distinctly.
4. Repeat the sequence of abdominal thrusts, finger sweep, and rescue breathing (attempt to ventilate) as long as necessary to remove the object from the obstructed airway.

Source: US Marine Corps

Stop when the subject resumes breathing. If they do not, move into rescue breathing and CPR if needed.

Training Standard

1. Describe the signs and symptoms of a choking victim.

2. Explain what to do if the victim can still cough.

3. Demonstrate delivering back blows.

4. Demonstrate abdominal thrusts on a conscious victim.

5. Demonstrate abdominal thrusts on an unconscious victim.

Tactical Wisdom

First Aid Manual

Chapter 6

Wounds

*He heals the brokenhearted
and binds up their wounds.*

Psalms 147:3

In an earlier chapter, we discussed applying a tourniquet and mentioned dressing wounds or bandaging them. These are important concepts and, in this chapter, we're going to discuss wounds and how to bandage & protect wounds.

Wounds are openings or damage to the skin and tissue underneath. They range from minor lacerations to burns, gunshots wounds, and traumatic amputations. Wounds are associated with trauma.

The first step in any wound is to stop the bleeding or burning.

Lacerations

A laceration is more commonly known as a cut. They range from superficial to deep and dangerous cuts. The danger from cuts is bleeding, as well as the potential for foreign objects to enter the cut and cause an infection. Sometimes, the cut is so deep that muscle and tissue beneath the skin is damaged as well. With some jagged cuts, there may be damage to surrounding tissue as well.

The first step in treating lacerations and cuts is to put on gloves or clean your hands. There is already enough risk of foreign bodies entering the cut and you don't need to add to it.

Use clean water and preferably gauze to clean the cut and pull it slightly apart to clean just inside the cut gently. A stream of water to flush things away (called irrigation) is far better than just wiping water on it. A syringe of water or something you can squirt from (water purification filter bag) will help.

If irrigation causes the wound to start bleeding again, use gauze and pressure to stop it.

After letting the wound air dry, you have to close it. You can use butterfly bandages or sterile strip-type bandages (like BandAids), Nu-Skin or super-glue, or even just medical tape in a pinch. Some deep wounds will require stitches, but stitches are beyond the scope of this manual. You should have someone on your medical team experienced in wound closure with stitches.

After closing the wound, cover it with a sterile dressing as described below. If the wound is on a joint, you may need to splint it to immobilize it so that it doesn't pull back open.

See the chapter on Bone & Joint Injuries for splinting.

Puncture Wounds

Anything that directly pierces the skin and makes a hole is a puncture wound. These would include stab wounds and gunshot wounds. My personal favorite, bayonet wounds, are also puncture wounds.

Since most of the damage is below the surface, they might not bleed as much as a laceration. A big risk is internal bleeding that doesn't exit the skin. Sometimes, like a splinter, the object that caused the puncture may still be inside, raising the risk of infection. If the puncture was in an area covered by clothing, pieces of dirty clothing inside the wound also pose an infection risk.

Wound cleaning becomes vital.

With small puncture wounds, encourage a little bleeding to clean the puncture. Use sterilized tweezers (either from heat or alcohol) to remove any large foreign objects. Then, clean the wound with soap and water, rinsing thoroughly with clean water after. Let the wound air dry, then cover and apply a dressing.

Some large puncture wounds may need to be "packed" with sterile gauze to promote healing. See the section below on Packing Wounds.

In a survival setting, a fishhook in the skin is a common injury. If the hook has not gone in past the barbed end, just pull it out. If the barb is imbedded, pulling the hook straight out will do significantly more damage and will be extremely painful.

Instead, gently push the hook though in a curving motion, until the barb pokes through the skin. Use snips or wire cutters to cut off the barb and pull the shank of the hook back out.

Then clean and dress the wound.

Abrasions

An abrasion is what we call a scrape. It is caused by something scraping across the skin and the skin gives before the object does.

Scrapes generally don't bleed much, but there is a risk of infection.

Clean the wound thoroughly with soap and water, and then rinse with clear water and dress the wound as described below.

Contusions

The contusion is a bruise. Generally, they are not very serious and only need minor treatment. Serious bruises should be looked at by the medical professionals on your team to make sure that they aren't hiding more serious injuries like broken bones.

Generally, treat bruises with an ice pack or something cold on top of it.

Blisters

Let's face it, a WROL situation is going to lead to a lot of walking. Blisters are a common problem with walking long distances. Blisters are also caused by friction or heat.

The best treatment for blisters is to protect them and let them resolve on their own by naturally draining. Protect blisters by covering them and surrounding them with Moleskin bandages.

If a blister must be drained because it is too painful to be left alone, you can drain it manually. Start by cleaning the affected area. Sterilize a needle in flame. Use the needle to poke a hole in the blister at the edge. Press out the fluid. Dress the wound like any other laceration or abrasion.

Burns

Burns range from minor to severe and can be excruciating as far as pain. There are three degrees of burns:

1. First Degree: Sunburn; minor burns. Redness.
2. Second Degree: A deeper burn that generally involves blisters. Protect the blisters from breaking to prevent infection.
3. Third Degree: Charred skin and blisters. This involves damage to deep tissue and requires advanced medical treatment.

For first- and second-degree burns, apply cool water or a cool wet cloth to cool. Let the wound air dry, and then cover loosely with a bandage. Do NOT apply ice.

For third-degree burns, use designated burn dressings to loosely cover the wound. If possible, elevate the burn above the level of the heart. Watch the person for shock and loosen all belts and remove any rings. Do NOT attempt to pull burned clothing from the skin. Allow your professional medical team to treat further.

If the burns were chemical burns, flush the area with water for at least 15 minutes. Change the victim's clothing as the chemical may still be on it.

Dressing Wounds

There is far more to it than just slapping a gauze pad on the wound.

We will start with commonly used trauma dressings, then work our way to some more creative methods. We'll talk about the ways to use a triangular bandage. While our main focus is on major trauma, we'll also discuss bandaging more everyday wounds as well.

Emergency Trauma Dressing

The Emergency Trauma Dressing or "ETD" is a dressing and a bandage all in one. They consist of a non-adherent pad to cover the wound directly and attached "tails" of bandaging material to wrap around the wound and bandage it with. They are meant to apply direct pressure to stop bleeding while also covering and protecting the wound. Modern versions, called "Israeli" bandages, have a plastic or metal bar for securing the ends of the bandage. Older versions require you to tie a square knot to secure them after putting them over the wound.

ETDs should be tried before tourniquets when you have time available.

Below are the steps for applying an ETD:

- Open the dressing package.
- Apply the dressing, white side down (sterile, nonadherent pad) directly over the wound.
- Wrap the elastic tail (bandage) around the extremity and run the tail through the plastic pressure bar, if it has one.
- Reverse the tail while applying pressure and continue to wrap the remainder of the tail around the extremity, while continuing to apply pressure directly over the wound.
- Secure the plastic closure bar to the last turn of the wrap or tie the bandage securely using a square knot.
- Check the emergency bandage to make sure that it is applied firmly enough to prevent slipping but not too tight.

Frequently check these dressings to make sure that the bleeding has stopped.

Remember: Always use the casualty's dressing first.

ETDs come in several different sizes. I recommend carrying a 4 inch and a 6-inch ETD.

Your team kit should have a variety of sizes for various scenarios and injuries.

Field Expedient ETD's

When you don't have a packaged ETD, you can make your own, using a Trauma Pad/ABD pad. These are sold as "Abdominal Pads" or "Trauma Pads". Place the pad directly over the wound and secure it in place by bandaging with elastic bandage or self-adhering bandages (elastic type).

Dressing Other Larger Wounds

Any other wound that is larger than what a band-aid can cover should be covered with gauze and then bandaged using elastic/self-adhering bandages.

There is no secret technique to bandaging, simply wrap the elastic/self-adhering bandage around the wound, and a little above/a little below the wound to keep the dressing in place and keep dirt out.

Wound Packing

Sometimes, a deep wound needs a little extra help to stop bleeding. We can apply direct pressure inside a wound by "packing" the wound. Always wear gloves when conducting wound packing.

Clean the wound as best you can, then open a gauze packet or gauze roll to get a good supply of gauze to fill the wound cavity. Pack the gauze tightly into the wound, being careful not to expand the wound while packing. Cover the packed wound with an ETD or a gauze pad and bandage.

Hemostatic Agents

Hemostatic agents are used in wounds to try and quicken the process of coagulation or clotting, stopping the bleeding sooner.

There are powder types and gauze that is impregnated with the hemostatic agent. The gauze type is preferred, because powders are harder to apply and may be blown off by the wind or washed away by rain/blood before you can dress the wound. Choose gauze types whenever you can.

Hemostatic agents are a SUPPLEMENT to direct pressure and pressure dressings, not a replacement. They are not magic. If you have a bleeding patient and you need to pack the wound as discussed above, use hemostatic gauze like QuikClot if you have it available.

There has been a lot of talk about hemostatic agents (chitosan) being derived from shellfish. While that is true, there have been ZERO cases of reported ill effects, even in people who have severe shellfish allergies. Newer generations of QuikClot are made from Kaolin, rather than shellfish derivatives.

The Triangular Bandage

The triangular bandage has been in use for a very long time and it's a versatile tool. You should have at least one in your IFAK and several in your team kit. As the name implies, it's a triangular piece of cloth (usually muslin) that can be used for various first aid purposes.

The shape lends itself to being used as a sling (more on that later) very easily.

You can fold it over or roll it up to make a long, flat bandage. The package generally contains safety pins to secure the sling or bandage, but you can also tie it in knots.

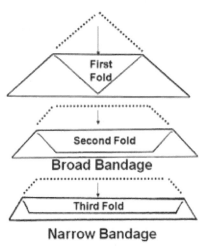

I recommend buying them in green or black, but white versions are out there as well. US military ones are green.

You can turn a shemagh into a triangular bandage by folding it diagonally. You can also fold it directly into a flat bandage. Another thing you can do with a shemagh is to tear it into strips for bandages.

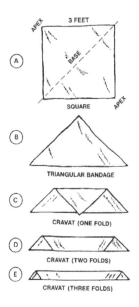

A — SQUARE (3 FEET, APEX, BASE, APEX)

B — TRIANGULAR BANDAGE

C — CRAVAT (ONE FOLD)

D — CRAVAT (TWO FOLDS)

E — CRAVAT (THREE FOLDS)

Minor Wounds

We carry a "Boo-Boo Kit" consisting of band-aid type bandages for covering small wounds. It's vital in a WROL situation that we don't neglect minor wounds. There is this "tough guy" image that leads to us not wanting a band-aid on our "boo-boo". That's DANGEROUS in a WROL environment, where advanced antibiotics to treat infections won't be available.

As soon as possible, clean the cut or scrape, apply a liberal amount of topical antibiotic or antiseptic, and then immediately cover it with an appropriate size/shape band-aid.

Carry more than you think you need. They cost you no weight and you'll be surprised at how many you might need. Make sure to include unique ones like fingertip and knuckle bandages. Have the right tool for the right job.

Closing Wounds

While suturing (putting in stitches) is beyond the scope of this manual, I urge you to get trained in how to do it. There are many training products available to help you learn how.

Stock items like butterfly bandages, New-Skin or similar adhesive, and even superglue in a pinch. These can all be used to close wounds to encourage healing.

Never apply any of these items until the bleeding has stopped. Butterfly strips should only be used on straight lacerations.

To apply butterfly strips, pinch the wound closed and apply the strips to the wound, about 1/8 of an inch apart. One they are in place; you can cover this with another dressing for cleanliness. After the first 48 hours, you can leave it exposed and it can get wet. Butterfly closures can be left on for up to 12 days.

For New-Skin or other glue-type adhesive bandages, hold the wound closed and spray it on or apply it with the nozzle/applicator. Re-apply as often as needed.

Wound Management

After bandaging, a wound should be cleaned once each day with soap and water. Apply antibiotic lotion or white petroleum and re-cover the wound. You don't need to clean with hydrogen peroxide or alcohol every day, but it's a good idea on the initial follow up to the original injury.

Deep wounds should be re-packed but wet the gauze before packing.

Bandaging

In general, bandaging is nothing more than covering your dressing, like a gauze pad, with some type of bandage. It could be self-conforming bandages, Ace-type bandages, a Triangular bandage, or really anything that can cover and protect the gauze pad that is covering the wound. We want to keep any medicines like antibiotics in and dirt out.

Cover with gauze pad

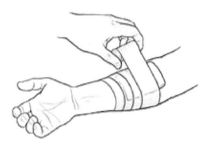

Bandage

To bandage joints like an ankle or a wrist, use a figure 8 pattern both above and below the joint.

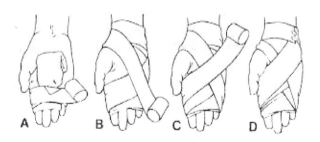

Figure 8 Bandage

Training Standard

- Describe the treatment for lacerations or cuts.

- Describe the treatment for puncture wounds.

- Describe the treatment for abrasions.

- Describe the treatment for bruises.

- Describe the treatment for blisters.

- Describe the three degrees of burns and the treatment for each.

- Demonstrate how to apply an emergency trauma dressing.

- Demonstrate how to apply a tourniquet.

- Describe wound packing.

- Explain the use of hemostatic agents.

- Demonstrate bandaging various wounds.

Tactical Wisdom

First Aid Manual

Chapter 7

Bites and Stings

Then the Lord sent venomous snakes among them; they bit the people and many Israelites died.

Numbers 21:6

While bites and stings constitute an annoyance today, they can be deadly in a WROL situation, with no access to advanced treatment. Some people are allergic, some insects carry diseases, and some snakes are venomous.

Bites and stings itch and that leads to scratching them open. Open wounds lead to infections, and you will have limited ability to treat infections. It's better to take quick action.

The first thing is for all members of your family or preparedness group to fully disclose any allergies to everyone else. It's important, because with some stings and bites, seconds matter.

Our best strategy here is to keep as much of our skin covered as possible. Yes, here comes the cargo shorts lecture. The majority of snake bites are because someone stepped on a snake, therefore, it's below the knee. If you are wearing good boots and long pants, the bite is unlikely to penetrate. Long pants and long sleeves also keep bugs off your skin, and therefore unable to bite.

In TW-01, I recommended buying surplus military uniforms and gear for a number of reasons. One of these is that the uniforms and some camping gear come pre-treated with insect repellent. You can also re-treat them. Wearing long pants "bloused" as US Marines do, prevents insects from getting under the clothing. Blousing involves wrapping an elastic band around the top of your boot and tucking the pants up under that band. It's better than just tucking them into your boots, as bugs can still find their way down if you tuck. Tucking your pants into your boots is a good second choice though.

Another preventative measure for both snakes and insects are leg gaiters. Gaiters are a waterproof covering that goes over your lower leg and boot and are attached to your boots in some way. They keep dirt, water, and snow off your pants, as well as insects. They are also abrasion and puncture resistant, stopping snake bites.

Never reach under logs or brush without visually checking first. This will prevent most snake and insect bites.

While bug sprays are fine, I recommend only natural ones, because of the odor. The other issue is that you will not be getting a resupply, so how will you maintain supplies? I recommend wipes over sprays, just because they are quieter and involve less wasted spray. The wipes are also biodegradable, so they can be buried after use.

In this book, we are not going to get hyper-specific on all types of creepy-crawly creatures. We will discuss general treatment. If a specific kind of insect or snake is in your area, learn to treat it.

Insects – Ticks/Mosquitoes

The most common bites we all get are mosquitoes, chiggers, no-see-ums, and flies. These are generally not dangerous and present mostly an annoyance, although mosquitoes are known to carry disease. These are best prevented with insect repellents and by keeping long pants/long sleeves covering as much of our skin as possible. They are treated with balms of calamine, camphor, or even oatmeal.

Natural bug repellents are lavender oil, garlic oil (works on ticks), citronella oil, and oil of lemon eucalyptus. Make sure you dilute these before applying directly to your skin.

Ticks are the real danger. Ticks carry many diseases including such favorites as Lyme disease and Rocky Mountain Spotted Fever. The reason that ticks are dangerous is that they burrow into your skin.

Ticks removed in less than 36 hours rarely transmit illness, so it's important to check for ticks regularly. There are tons of old wives' tales about how to remove a tick, but it's best to just use tweezers, as close to the bite as possible. Pull straight up with steady pressure and the tick will usually let go.

After removal, immediately clean the area with soap and water or alcohol. Watch the site for infection. Starting 3 to 5 days of Doxycycline (100mg) twice a day is a good idea when you remove a tick that has been on you for an unknown length of

71

time. Should a rash develop, treat with Doxycycline 100mg for 5 to 14 days (or Amoxicillin 500 – ask me how I know).

If a fever develops with a tick bite, treat for 10 to 21 days with Doxycycline 100mg twice day or 14 to 21 days with Amoxicillin 500mg twice a day. Continue the treatment even if the symptoms subside.

Insects – Bees/Wasps

With stinging insects, it's important to be careful when removing a stinger. If the stinger is still inside the victim, don't use tweezers. Using tweezers will force more venom into the sting. Scrape the stinger out with a knife blade or something similar, scraping away from the site. Remember that wasps can both bite and sting.

Some people (like me) are very allergic to bee stings. These people should have Epi-Pens. This is not medical advice, but even expired Epi-Pens can be helpful. Generally, they are still full-strength for up to nine months after (in fact, the FDA allows using them that long). After nine months, they begin to lose potency. However, in an anaphylactic reaction, some efficacy is better than none. We are talking about an environment where you can't just run out and get a new one. Never use an auto-injector that appears cloudy.

One study showed that after 12 months past expiration, EpiPens retained 95% of their original dose and after 30 months, they still retained over 90%. Don't be so hung up on expiration dates for EpiPens, especially in a full collapse. Reminder, this book is not medical advice and should not be treated as such.

For most bee stings, removing the stinger, washing it with soap and water, and a cold compress is treatment enough. Topical pain relief creams (hydrocortisone or calamine) can be used for discomfort.

Allergic reactions may require Benadryl or an Epi-Pen if severe.

A paste of baking soda and water or mustard (yes, mustard) applied to the bee sting may alleviate itching and pain. Remember, itching the sting raises the risk of infection, especially in an austere/disaster environment.

Spider Bites

Spider bites happen about 3 million times a year in the US. Most are no different than other insect bites, resulting in a red bump that itches. Again, the biggest risk is infection.

Spiders don't bite unless threatened, so avoid areas where spiders like to live like attics, basements, and dark corners. Try not to disturb any spiders you find.

The treatment for most spider bites is to clean the area with soap and water and apply ice packs or a cold compress. Analgesics (Acetaminophen) or NSAID's (Non-steroidal anti-inflammatory drugs like Ibuprofen or Naproxen) can be taken for pain and inflammation.

Some spiders are poisonous, like the black widow, the brown recluse, and the hobo spider, to name a few. Learn what spiders are poisonous in your area. Symptoms of bites from these include difficulty breathing, painful muscle cramps, and a severe headache. They can also cause flu-like symptoms and swelling.

Even these bites are rarely fatal, except in children. Elevate the injury, apply hydrocortisone or calamine, and treat with pain medication or anti-inflammatories. Monitor the patient's breathing and heart rate.

Clean the bite twice a day until the recovery is complete. Don't use alcohol or peroxide on spider bites, as that slows down healing. A small amount of petroleum jelly on the bite can help. You can also cover the bite with a Band-Aid.

Snake Bites

Just like spiders, most snakes in North America are not poisonous. There are a few that are, and we will discuss treating those bites. Most bites, even by venomous snakes, in North America are not fatal.

Like everything else, prevention is the best medicine. Most snake bites are caused by someone stepping on a snake. Snakes are generally reclusive and will go the other way when they sense your presence. Never try to handle snakes.

Quality boots, sturdy pants, and leg gaiters reduce the risk of a snake biting you.

The biggest issue with snake bites is not knowing exactly what kind of snake did the biting. Some non-venomous ones look like venomous ones. We begin treatment for all snake bites the same way:

1. Wash the area.
2. Keep the affected area still and lower than the heart.
3. Remove all rings or other constricting things in case of swelling.

4. You can apply a cold compress or wet dressing to alleviate discomfort.

Because there are two different types of venom, we have to monitor the patient. Pit vipers (rattlesnakes, cottonmouth/water moccasins, and copperheads) affect the victim's blood, while coral snakes, sea snakes, cobras, and kraits impact the central nervous system.

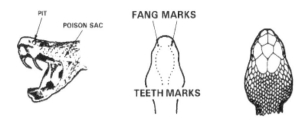

Figure 6-2. Characteristics of poisonous pit viper.

Source: USMC First Aid Manual

Watch for the victim to have swelling, convulsions, and an altered mental state. While most are not fatal, they can be. Management of pain and symptoms is the best we can do in an austere environment.

Generally, pit vipers cause bruising and bleeding that will not clot well and coral snakes (and their cousins) cause difficulty breathing, altered mental state/convulsions, loss of coordination, and paralysis.

While we probably won't have antivenin available, we can give pain medications, antibiotics, and maintain a watch on the victim's vitals. Give CPR or rescue breathing if needed. Keep the victim calm and resting if possible.

Place a constricting band one or two inches above and below the bite. This should not completely shut off the blood flow like a tourniquet. You should be able to slip a finger underneath the band.

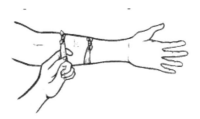

Figure 6-8. Constricting band.

Source: USMC First Aid Manual

One way to see if the venom is spreading in pit viper bites is to draw a circle around the wound. Check later and see of the swelling and redness or bruising has extended outside the circle.

A lot of the "common knowledge" about snake bite treatment is 100% false. For example:

1. Do not apply a tourniquet.
2. Do not attempt suction.
3. Do not cut open a snake bite.
4. Do not apply ice to a snake bite.

Scorpion Bites

Scorpion bites or stings generally don't cause serious reactions except for anaphylactic shock in people allergic to them. This is exceptionally rare.

Symptoms of a scorpion bite are:

1. Local pain and swelling.
2. Nausea and vomiting.
3. Serious cases: blurry vision and a racing heart, along with muscle twitches and drooling.

Treatment for a scorpion bite includes:

1. Wash the site.
2. Treat the pain with medication.
3. Benadryl can help with symptoms.
4. Monitor for anaphylactic reaction.
   a. Treat with Epi-Pen and Benadryl.
   b. Monitor vitals and be prepared to perform rescue breathing or CPR.

Animal Bites

This includes human bites, which are not out of the question. It does NOT include Zombie bites; you are on your own.

Generally, treat all animal bites as wounds. Wash the area thoroughly and irrigate with water. Apply antibiotics and give a preventative dose of Amoxicillin or Penicillin, whichever you have.

Training Standard

- Describe preventative measure for bites and stings.

- Describe the treatment for mosquito bites.

- Describe the treatment for tick bites.

- Describe the treatment for bee stings.

- Describe the treatment for anaphylactic shock (allergic reaction).

- Describe the treatment for spider bites.

- Describe the treatment for snake bites.

- Describe the treatment for scorpion bites and stings.

- Describe the treatment for all other bites.

Tactical Wisdom

First Aid Manual

Chapter 8

Muscle, Bone, & Joint Injuries

Let me hear joy and gladness;
let the bones you have broken rejoice.

Psalm 51:8

As I said earlier, I begin every Defensive Firearms Course with these two questions:

1. Raise your hand if you've ever been in a gunfight.
2. Raise your hand if you've ever fallen down.

Sure, it gets a few laughs, but any time I get people together to talk about first aid, all they want to talk about is gunshots. I ask them to show me their first aid kit, and all they have are things to treat gunshots or major trauma.

I've got some bad news. In a WROL situation or a disaster, a broken ankle can become fatal. You can't walk, and therefore you can't eat. You can't go and get treatment from anyone else either. Sprains are just as bad.

In this chapter, we'll cover how to diagnose and treat these injuries. Remember, we aren't just stabilizing to wait for transport, we likely have to do it all ourselves. Again, we are talking about austere treatment, not modern "medical treatment within an hour" standards, so bear with me.

Let's begin with the two main categories of injury. Sprains involve stretching or tearing the ligaments around a joint. Fractures are breaks in the bone to varying degrees.

Fractures can be open, meaning breaking through the skin, or closed. A "greenstick" fracture is one that is not a complete break. Oblique fractures are breaks that are diagonal to some degree. A transverse fracture is a straight-line break completely through.

Sprains

As mentioned above, these are stretching or tearing ligaments around a joint. These are common hiking injuries when you twist an ankle. They are also common when people improperly break their fall with their hands, or they fall improperly on the shoulder.

Diagnosing a sprain is simple. There are four things to look for:

1. Joint pain.
2. Stiffness in the joint.
3. Swelling.
4. Discoloration such as redness but especially bruising.

We treat sprains using the RICE acronym:

R	Rest
I	Ice
C	Compression
E	Elevation

Have the patient rest, if possible, and raise the limb. If you have ice or an ice pack, apply it. You could use a cold compress if you don't have ice packs. Use an elastic bandage to compress the site of the injury.

If the patient absolutely has to move, such as in a combat or evasion situation, apply compression and you can do the rest later. Just make sure some rest and elevation are arranged for later.

You can't hurry along recovery from a sprain, but you can certainly lengthen it by not allowing rest.

The only exception is ankle sprains. There is evidence that early use of the ankle leads to better and faster healing. Tough it out, Chief. Crying is OK, quitting is not.

Don't splint sprains, an elastic bandage is sufficient compression.

Fractures

Generally, fractures are fairly obvious. Body parts are bent at angles that are not possible when the bone is intact. Contrary to popular belief, X-Rays are generally not required to diagnose fractures; they are used to confirm a diagnosis.

There are several symptoms for the non-obvious fractures:

1. Swelling or bruising over the site.
2. Deformity at the site.
3. Pain that gets worse when the area is touched or moved.
4. Inability to bear or lift weight.
5. Loss of function in the area.

Questions you can ask the patient include:

1. Did you hear a snap, pop, or crack?
2. Did you lose function immediately or did it slowly decrease (fracture is immediate)?
3. Can you move it?

Reduction and immobilization are the ways to treat a fracture. Without access to pharmaceuticals, this is going to be painful.

Reduction refers to putting the bone back in place. With surgery most likely not being an option, we're going to have to add the caveat of "as best we can". We may not be able to, without surgical pins or traction, put the pieces back perfectly. We are stuck with an 1800s level of ability here. This doesn't mean all is lost; people survived and recovered from broken bones in the 1800s.

Put the broken bone back in place as best you can, treating the pain however you can. Again, having access to pharmaceuticals is best, but in the 1800s whiskey helped. Whiskey can help with most things.

With open fractures, first clean the exposed bone as best you can (betadine or iodine solutions help). Normally, we wouldn't put the bone back in place, we'd leave that for a treatment facility. We don't have a treatment facility, so you may have to reduce the open fracture in the field, dress the wound, and then splint the fracture.

Once we have reduced the fracture, immobilization comes next. To accomplish this, we use splints. A SAM splint is a moldable splint we use to hold a fracture in place in the field, but we may have to use it for long term field care, because we won't have material for a plaster cast. Try to immobilize the joint above and below the fracture when splinting.

You can also use sticks with a triangular bandage or compression/ACE bandage to immobilize a fracture. Use whatever you have at hand to hold the recovering bones in place. Finger splints can be stored for use on finger fractures or tape can be used to hold a finger or toe straight along the one next to it.

There is a SAM Medical YouTube channel with videos on how to use the SAM Splint. The videos go into great detail of splinting every type of fracture with a SAM Splint. I highly recommend watching them.

If you have boards available, they can be padded with gauze and then used as splints as well.

The biggest factor in healing broken bones is time. The body will repair the damage on its own, but it will take time. Some fractures can take up to a year to heal. The best thing we can do is reduce them (set them in place) and immobilize the bones. Time does the rest for the majority of fractures.

Dislocations

A dislocation is when the joint has bones that have popped out of place. They are much easier to fix right after they happen. Reducing a dislocation immediately dramatically reduces (but not eliminates) the pain felt and can make someone able to function as a member of the team much more quickly.

The symptoms include:

1. Obvious deformity (compare left to right, etc.)

2. Decreased range of motion

To reduce finger and toe dislocations, apply traction (pull the finger or toe) and then tape to the one next to it.

Shoulders are reduced by using a technique first documented in 1870 called "Kocher's Method". It may actually be 3000 years old and is relatively painless. Bend the arm 90 degree at the elbow and hold the upper arm firmly against the side of the chest. Rotate the hand outward about 75 or 80 degrees, until you feel some resistance. Lift the upper arm from elbow straight forward as far as you can, then twist the shoulder until their hand is near the opposite shoulder. This should reduce the dislocation with relatively little pain.

A secondary method is to pad the armpit, have them lay down. Then, place a foot in the arm pit while gently pulling the arm until the shoulder slides back in.

No matter which technique is used, sling the arm afterwards. Simply tie the triangular bandage around their neck and place the arm in it.

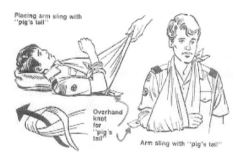

Source: Boy Scouts of America

For the sternoclavicular joint or collarbone, near the center top of the chest, have the patient lay down. Place a roll of something between the shoulder blades and press down, while pulling back the arm slowly on the affected side.

When it's the ankle, have the knee bent, while you use traction (pulling) slowly to bring the ankle back into place.

Knees should only be done as a last resort. They should be done by applying traction gently to the knee, in a rearward direction (pulling it back against the way it goes).

These are some very basic pieces of advice for putting some of the more common joints back in place. When in doubt, use gradual yet firm traction.

Training Standard

1. Describe how to diagnose and treat sprains.

2. Describe how to diagnose and treat fractures.

3. Describe how to diagnose and treat dislocations.

4. Demonstrate splinting.

5. Demonstrate how to apply a sling.

Tactical Wisdom

First Aid Manual

Chapter 9

Environmental Injuries

The tempest comes out from its chamber,
the cold from the driving winds.

Job 37:9

The environment is every bit as dangerous to us as other people are. If we are not sufficiently prepared, we can become casualties to the heat and cold. I remember as a young Marine, I was assigned to attend some cold weather training. I felt that as a Michigan Native, I was fully prepared for anything that the Mountain Warfare School could throw at me. A few days later, I lay shivering on the side of a mountain making bargains with God. The number one cause of environmental injuries is over-confidence in our skills and gear.

In this chapter, we will deal with cold injuries, heat injuries, and immersion in cold water, as well as some more specific environmental illnesses. We'll do our best to prevent them first, but we will cover treatment options.

COLD INJURIES

Shelter becomes a vital issue in the cold. The first preventative tip is to learn how to quickly throw up shelters from harsh winter weather. Keeping warm is our number one goal, so when we build winter shelters, having a way to insulate our bodies from the cold ground is absolutely vital. If you don't have a pad, bring in branches or whatever you can find to keep from laying directly on the cold ground.

You need to stay dry. The body loses heat around 24 times faster when wet, so do everything you can to stay dry or to dry off quickly. Having a change of base layers and a microfiber towel can save your life. Waterproofing your ruck or patrol pack is also vital.

Prevention begins with eating and drinking properly in the cold. You will need more calories when operating outside in a cold environment. This is why the US issues special cold weather MRE's with more calories than normal. Your body is a furnace and to heat effectively it needs sufficient fuel. The US Naval Medical Command recommends 4,500 calories a day for troops active outdoors in a cold weather environment.

Outdoors in the winter you should be eating something small every 2 hours.

It's easier to get dehydrated in the cold than in the heat because you don't realize how much water you lose. When on the move, you need about 8 quarts of water a day, and when static, you can drop to 6 quarts (guidelines from the USMC Mountain Warfare Training Center).

When the British fought the Falkland Island War, the fighting was in the winter in the southern hemisphere and in a rough climate. It gets cold in the South Atlantic. Constipation was a major issue with the British troops, and both diet and dehydration played a role. Military meals are notoriously low in fiber, and you need fiber. The lack of fiber and poor water discipline led to a decrease in combat effectiveness due to constipation. I told you earlier that constipation can kill you.

The next area of cold injury prevention concerns our clothing and equipment. You don't want giant, heavy layers, as was taught in the old days. You need to be able to layer with lightweight layers that are easy to put on or take off. The clothes need to be durable, and they need to offer protection against the wind and rain.

As usual, I look to the USMC's cold weather clothing system. Surplus gear has had millions of dollars spent on research to develop it for the harshest conditions on the planet. I know, all the cool-guy YouTube experts with their affiliate links will tell you all about the latest and highly expensive gear, but if you're on a budget, military surplus is the way to go. When buying surplus, try to get "new old stock", meaning it has never been issued.

Remember, we use acronyms to sound cool and sound like insiders, so the acronym for how to wear our clothes is "COLD".

C	Clean – Keep your clothing clean.
O	Overheating – Avoid overheating.
L	Loose/Layers – Wear clothing loose and in layers.
D	Dry – Keep your clothing dry.

In cold weather, you should always carry a clothing repair kit and a shelter repair kit. This will enable you to repair your gear quickly to keep it functioning.

<u>Hypothermia</u>

Hypothermia is when your core body temperature falls to 95 degrees Fahrenheit (35 Celsius for the Crown's Subjects). It is fatal in about 50% of severe cases. It can cause a heart attack. Don't think it's only limited to severe cold either, 50% of cases occur when the ambient temperature is 50 F or higher.

Hypothermia occurs more often in males than females, almost 3 to 1 (probably because men do dumb things and women are smarter). The elderly are also more susceptible to hypothermia.

Note that shivering (muscle activity to generate heat) begins when the body cools to around 97 degrees (36 C) and then ceases at around 85-90 (30-34 C).

The symptoms are:

- 98-95 F: Mild shivering, feeling cold, and impaired fine motor skills.
- 95-92 F: Violent shivering, difficulty speaking, sluggish thinking, and some amnesia. May have large muscle coordination loss.

- 92-86 F: No more shivering – muscles become rigid. Exposed skin is blue/puffy. Jerky movements.
- 85-81 F: Coma, loss of reflexes, possible arrythmia (ventricular for you medical types).
- Below 78 F: Cardiac and respiratory failure.
- Paradoxical undressing: When the body tries to rush heat to the core, some victims feel that the skin is hot and then undress completely. This is a sure sign of hypothermia.

The treatment of hypothermia:

- Remove wet clothing and replace it with dry clothing. Create a vapor barrier to prevent heat loss. Wrapping the them in two plastic trash bags can do this, as can bubble wrap.
- If they have altered consciousness, give nothing by mouth. Absolutely do NOT give alcohol to hypothermia patients, despite what they do in the movies.
- Since we won't be able to send the victim to the hospital in a WROL situation (you should in the current world) – we need to put them into a sleeping bag to rewarm. You should have a non-hypothermic person pre-warm the sleeping bag for several minutes first. You can place heated water bottles in the sleeping bag with them to rewarm. If they are conscious with no altered states, give warm fluids like broth.
  - o If needed, have two volunteers place the cold casualty between them for shared warmth.
- If you have a warm bath available, that's a good rewarming strategy. The water should be at 104-108 F.
- If you have trained medical staff, warmed IV solutions can be used, but that is beyond the scope of this manual.

Frostbite

Frostbite is the literal freezing of tissue. Frostbite generally occurs after a long-term exposure to sub-freezing temperatures but can also happen with high wind-chill. Generally, it occurs after more than 12 hours outside in freezing weather. Parts of the body with less muscle mass are at greater risk of frostbite (fingers, toes, ears, etc.).

The symptoms of frostbite include:

- Pain and discomfort in the affected tissue.
- Loss of sensation.
- Skin looks white and bloodless.
- Little to no capillary refill.
- In minor cases, blisters can form.

Treating frostbite in the field:

- First, if there is a chance of immediate refreezing, don't attempt to thaw the injured part until there is not. In other words, get them out of the cold first.
- Rapid rewarming is the best treatment. Immerse the body part in circulating (moving) warm water of 104-108 F for 40 to 60 minutes.
- Slow rewarming leads to more damage from ice reforming.
- Also, rubbing with snow, an old treatment, enhances tissue damage, as does rewarming next to an open fire.
- For longer-term healing after thawing, aloe vera gel can help, along with NSAID (anti-inflammatory) drugs.

As with most things, prevention is far better than treatment. Prevent frostbite by:

- Wearing mittens rather than gloves, as mittens are MUCH warmer. Again, US military ECWS mittens are the way to go. Waterproof and cozy.
- Don't dress to be WARM, dress to be comfortably cool.
- Since you lose the most heat (30%) from the head, if your feet are cold, put on a hat.
- Remember COLD, above. Don't wear tight-fitting clothes. While they look fabulous at the ski resort and on Instagram, they restrict blood flow, which warms the skin.
- Never, not even when "double dog dared" like in A Christmas Story, touch metals with skin in extremely low temperatures.
  - Since men are dumb (see above), should this happen like it did to Ralphie's poor friend in A Christmas Story, pour a warm liquid over the metal to thaw your flesh.

Immersion Foot

Let's face it, WROL life will involve long periods of watch-standing or standing still in a cold and wet environment. In this case, immersion foot can occur after 12 hours of exposure to a wet and cold (less than 50 F) environment. Blood circulation is reduced because your body is trying to reduce heat loss. This leads to the tissue damage we call immersion foot. While it mostly affects feet, don't let the name fool you, it can affect your hands as well.

The symptoms of immersion foot are:

- Numbness and potential cramps above the injury.
- The skin becomes increasingly pale, turning mottled, and then blue gray in color.
- Bruising and blisters can develop.

We can treat immersion foot in the field with these steps:

- Pat the area dry (do not rub).
- Gently re-warm the area affected.
- Elevate the extremity.
- Give bed rest (off the feet).
- DO NOT treat with immersion in warm water as we did with frostbite.
- Gangrene can develop, so monitor the patient.

Submersion in Water

I was originally going to say submersion in cold water, but the overwhelming majority of water occurring in the world has a temperature of 92 F or lower, so all water is cold water for our purposes. Immersion injuries are caused by the rapid immersion in water of humans.

When we hit the water unexpectedly, like falling through the ice, first we experience shock, then panic which leads to a violent struggle to get out of it. During this struggle, we gulp in air or water, which only increases our panic. Eventually, humans lose consciousness from hypoxia (lack of oxygen). The gag reflex then relaxes, and our lungs fill with water.

There are purely academic arguments over wet drowning and dry drowning, but in the end, both lead to death from asphyxiation, so there is no point in hashing over the differences here for our purposes. Dead is dead. We also won't get into the physiological differences between fresh water and saltwater drowning. Drowning is drowning.

Immersion victims are highly susceptible to hypothermia as water conducts heat away from your body 25 times faster than air does. Total body hypothermia is quick.

Immersion syndrome is a cardiac arrest brought on by the shock of entering very cold water. Cold water immersion also quickly leads to fatigue and poor decision-making ability.

Treatment for submersion:

- First, provide CPR if needed. You should conduct CPR with anyone without a pulse or respiration pulled from the water. People have survived after 66 minutes submerged in cold water. Make the attempt. No one is dead until they are warm and dead.
- Re-warm the victim using the above techniques once respiration and circulation have been restored.
- Getting them out of wet clothes and into sleeping bag rewarming is key.
- Expect near drowning victims to vomit.
- In a current world situation, patients should be checked out in a hospital and observed in the hospital for 6-8 hours.

Cold Water Survival

There are several techniques that can improve your chances of survival in cold water. This is a partial list, meant to help prevent submersion injuries.

- If the shore is more than a half mile away, don't attempt to swim it. The average person can't swim more than 1000 meters in 50 F water. Swimming rapidly increases heat loss. When we went fishing on Lake Superior, which is about 35 F, my grandfather showed me how close the shore was, but warned me that I would never make it, so staying with the boat was a better idea. This man survived the sinking of the USS Indianapolis and days in the water, so I'll take his word for it.
- Learn to tread water as calmly as you can.
- "Drown Proofing", while not preferred in cold water, can decrease your energy expenditure. Drown proofing is floating face down with your arms spread, only taking your head out of the water for breaths. This does expose your head to heat loss.
- As uncool as it is to wear a personal flotation device, they do save lives. In WROL water-borne operations, have them available.
  - If wearing a PFD, you can use the HELP position, called the Heat Escape Lessening Posture.
    - Cross your arms across the body, hugging yourself tight.
    - Bring the knees up to the chest and cross the ankles.
    - This can be tiring but it is warming.
- If there is more than one person in the water, huddling can share warmth. Consider it water spooning.
  - Put any children and elderly in the middle.

<u>Water Rescue</u>

When considering water rescue, we use the following memory aid: Reach & Pull, Throw, Tow, and (as a last resort) Go.

- If the person is conscious and close, hold out something for them to grab on to. This could even be a floating rope tossed to them.
- Throw something that floats as close to them as you can, giving them something to hold on to until rescue can be organized.
- Tow – Once they have the floating object to help stay afloat, find a way to tow them to shore.
- Go – As a last resort if these don't work or the person is unresponsive, go to them if you are a strong swimmer trained in water rescue.

This might seem harsh, but reality often is. If you aren't a strong swimmer, two drowned people is worse than one. Sometimes, you can't save them. Prepare for that possibility.

I've said this my whole life: There is no excuse for an adult not knowing how to swim and to swim strongly. You can't claim to be into preparedness if you can't swim. You're FAR more likely to fall into the water on any given day than you are to face a battalion of Chinese soldiers. Learn to swim and stop making excuses for why you haven't. From a WROL life perspective, you are more likely to need to cross a river than to need to clear a building. Please learn how to swim.

Heat Injuries

Overheating also causes injury. If your body can't regulate its temperature due to excessive heat or exertion, you are in danger of serious heat injury. We'll talk a bit about prevention and then some treatments for specific illnesses. It is far easier to prevent heat illnesses rather than treat them, because while we can start a fire in the cold, we can't turn down the Sun.

Heat illnesses are caused by excessive heat & humidity, issues with your body's cooling systems, or strenuous activity without adequate fluid intake or electrolyte replacement.

Your body regulates its heat by shedding it into the environment (radiation or convection) and by sweating (evaporation). When it can't keep up or is compromised by other infections or illnesses, heat injuries happen.

Factors that contribute include heat for several days, other illnesses, and poor water intake. Never rely on thirst to tell you when to drink. The average person doesn't drink nearly enough water.

Another important factor is that most heat illnesses occur in the morning, probably due to thinking it can't happen early before it gets hot out.

Preventing Heat Illness

- You need to be drinking 6 to 8 quarts of water, and even more when exerting yourself.
- If available, use fluid or electrolyte replacement beverages. Stock up on Gatorade packets or similar, and products like Liquid IV.

The early signs are cognitive changes like confusion and impaired physical ability. Watch for these and take action to cool these people down and get fluids into them.

Heat Syncope

This is simply fainting in the heat and happens most often when people are standing still with their legs locked. Encourage anyone standing in a hot environment to flex their legs to encourage blood flow and to sit down if they feel faint.

Fainting usually responds well to horizontal positioning (in other words, people recover quickly when laying down). Let anyone who faints rest while laying down in a cool, shaded area. Give fluids by mouth (water/electrolytes).

Heat Cramps

Heat cramps are spasms caused by the loss of salt in the muscles from sweating. Although you might be drinking plenty of water, you aren't replacing salt that way.

To treat these casualties, let them rest in a cool and shaded area. Stretching and massaging the cramps gently can help. Heat cramps respond fastest to salt solutions. Put ¼ to ½ a teaspoon of salt in a 1-quart canteen and have them SIP (not gulp) it. If you have a person trained in IV therapy, isotonic saline 0.9% NaCL might be needed for severe cases.

Heat Exhaustion

When your body is both dehydrated and has lost a lot of salt, the body develops low blood pressure and heat exhaustion follows. Heat exhaustion is tricky because it can develop over a few days as well. For example, while one day of poor hydration won't exhaust you, a deficit for three straight days WILL. Hydrate and take in salt.

The symptoms of heat exhaustion are:

- Dizziness
- Headache
- Fatigue
- Irritability & anxiety
- Nausea/vomiting
- Chills
- Heat cramps
- Profuse sweating

A trained medic examining the casualty would find tachycardia (fast and weak pulse), hyperventilation (fast breathing) and hypotension (low blood pressure). The body temperature may be normal or elevated.

Treating it involves hydration and lowering the body temperature:

- Lay them down in a cool (as cool as you can) and shaded area.
- Sprinkle them with water and fan the person (palm fronds and grapes optional).
- If you have ice packs, put them over large blood vessels near the surface (brachial/femoral).
- Toweling of the skin will lead to more sweating and better evaporation to cool them.
- If they are alert, rehydrate orally with cool water or Liquid IV/electrolyte mixes. Try to give 2 liters over the first 2 hours.

- If they are not alert, a trained medic can rehydrate via IV using LR (Ringer's Lactate) if you have it available.
- Let them rest and rehydrate for the next 24 to 36 hours.
- In a non-WROL situation, transport them to medical care immediately, trying to cool them during transport.

<u>Heat Stroke</u>

This is the most dangerous and serious of the heat injuries. It means that the body's cooling system has completely failed. The body continues to heat and cannot cool itself at all.

A clinical diagnosis of heat stroke requires three things: a core temperature of over 104 F (41 C for Crown loyalists), an altered mental status, and a cessation of sweating. However, since early treatment is the key, you should ALWAYS treat for heat stroke whenever someone passes out in the heat.

Heat Stroke Symptoms:

- Headache
- Shortness of breath
- Nausea/vomiting
- Low blood pressure
- Hot red skin
- Dry mouth
- Constricted pupils
- Tachycardia
- Core temperature over 104 F/41 C
- Weakness & dizziness
- Confused/aggressive/combative
- Seizures

Treating Heat Stroke:

- The rapid reduction of core temperature to 102 F or lower is key. Do this with a cool water bath (or ice water), pouring water over the person or hosing them down (the Navy used to do this to us at MCRD San Diego while we ran), fanning them, and placing ice pack if you have them at the neck, armpits, groin, forehead, and chest.
- Maintain the ABC's (airway/breathing/circulation).
- Monitor their temperature.
- If you have the skill and capability, infuse with Ringer's Lactate or Saline via IV at 500cc/hour for 4 hours.
- In a current-world scenario, transport to medical care immediately.

Altitude Illnesses

Everyone is susceptible to altitude illnesses. Prior ascents of mountains is no guarantee, nor is exceptionally good aerobic fitness. The truth is that science doesn't fully understand the physiological stresses high altitude has on us or why it impacts some differently than others.

We're going to talk about prevention and early detection of Acute Mountain Sickness (AMS), which is the precursor to two other altitude illnesses.

We can work to prevent AMS by having a gradual ascent, rather than trying to rush up and over mountains like they do in the movies. Don't ascend more than 3,000 feet in a single day up to 14,000 feet. After 14,000 feet, never climb more than 1,000 feet a day.

I know we've said it before, but drink water. Avoid alcohol or sedatives, as well as smoking (you won't be smoking post-WROL anyway). Eat many more carbs (about 70% of your calories should be carbs) than normal when in a high-altitude environment. Avoid over-exertion.

Use a "work high, sleep low" process. In other words, do your work and exertion slightly higher than you sleep. Drop down a bit before going to sleep to reduce the stress on your body.

<u>Acute Mountain Sickness</u>

The three most common symptoms of AMS are headache, nausea, and vomiting. According to the Lake Louise Consensus, headache must be present with other symptoms to diagnose AMS. Other symptoms include dizziness, drowsiness, malaise (laziness), weakness, insomnia, and anorexia (not wanting to eat).

To properly treat and manage AMS, it's important first to note that in most cases, AMS symptoms will resolve themselves within 1-2 days. Other steps include:

- No further ascent and assign light duty.
- Aspirin or Tylenol for headaches and no smoking.
- Encourage them to hyperventilate from time to time (breathing into a bag can help).
- If none of this helps in the first 2 days, descend 1,000 to 3,000 feet. This should resolve it quickly.

<u>High Altitude Cerebral Edema (HACE)</u>

HACE is a swelling of the brain. It occurs most often over 12,000 feet, but it can occur as low as 8,000 feet. It is the progression of AMS to the next level. If you don't slow down when you develop AMS and keep going, you WILL develop HACE.

The signs and symptoms begin with those listed for AMS. Additional signs of HACE include:

- Loss of coordination and balance called ataxia.
- Personality changes and mental state changes like poor judgment, stupor, and possibly a coma.
- Confusion, hallucinations, behavioral changes, convulsions, and weariness.
- Extremity paralysis.

It's important to note that you need to educate all your people about these symptoms, as most will only be noticed by the person experiencing them. Encourage them to report these symptoms and let them know there is no shame in having health issues.

Now, normally the treatment is evacuation to a medical facility ASAP. We're not going to have that luxury, so we need to catch it at the AMS level or soon after (early detection is KEY). Try to catch it at the ataxia or mental status change level.

Fatalities can occur within a few hours.

Make the person comfortable and begin an immediate descent. If you have oxygen, give it immediately in a high concentration.

For the paramedics, nurses, and doctors reading this, I am fully aware of the pharmacological treatment routes, but they are WAY beyond the scope of this manual. For the rest of you: Get a dedicated team medic who understands pharmacology.

<u>High Altitude Pulmonary Edema (HAPE)</u>

HAPE is the filling of the lungs with fluid for various reasons beyond the scope of this manual. It's important to note that it rarely occurs below 12,000 feet and occurs in 1-2% of people brought RAPIDLY to 12,000 feet (in other words: SLOW DOWN). HAPE occurs within 2-4 days of the ascent.

AMS occurs prior to HAPE in most cases. Again, catch things at the AMS level to head off more serious issues.

Things that increase the risk of HAPE are a high rate of ascent, sleeping very high, high levels of exertion, and HAPE impacts males more than females (again, because women are smarter and know their limits).

The signs and symptoms of HAPE begin to appear within 2-4 days of arrival at a high altitude. The early signs are a dry cough (generally at night), mild chest pain, difficulty breathing under exertion (especially walking uphill), decreased performance and need for more recovery time. Peripheral cyanosis or blue fingers and toes is another sign.

Signs of a more serious case are difficulty breathing while resting, cough with pink, frothy output, rapid pulse & respiration, crackling that be heard while listening, and mental status changes/ataxia (see HACE above).

It is urgent that you immediately descend 2,000-3,000 feet. Fatalities can occur within 6-12 hours in serious cases of HAPE. If you catch it early enough, the descent of 2,000-3,000 feet can fix the entire problem.

Carry them down the descent, as exertion makes the issue worse. If you have oxygen available, give them high-flow oxygen while descending.

NOTE ON HACE & HAPE: Descent is the MOST IMPORTANT treatment for both illnesses. Do it as soon as you can.

Training Standard

1. Explain the acronym COLD.

2. Explain hypothermia and how to treat it.

3. Explain frostbite and how to treat it.

4. List the treatment steps for water immersion.

5. List ways to prevent heat illnesses.

6. Explain heat exhaustion and how to treat it.

7. Explain heat stroke and how to treat it.

8. List the symptoms of Acute Mountain Sickness (AMS).

9. Explain the best immediate action step for all altitude illnesses.

Tactical Wisdom

First Aid Manual

Chapter 10

Psychological Emergencies

Cast all your anxiety on him,
because he cares for you...

1 Peter 5:7

Having the entire world collapse and returning to the Bronze Age will be stressful. People will have difficulty adjusting. Heck, imagine not being able to scroll Twitter to fall asleep. How many people use Facebook to feel better about themselves? I know I'm making light of it, but this is serious stuff. A lot of people will be unable to function without the internet or electricity. They will have to deal with grief from the loss of loved ones.

The threat of and daily exposure to violence will cause stress. This is important, because a lot of folks in the preparedness community believe that they will be living out some sort of Little House on the Prairie cosplay and that's just unrealistic. Even in the days of pioneers, there were bandits, native war bands, and general brigandry to worry about (that's a word that needs more use – brigandry).

Think about the sheer number of people on drugs for neurological issues. Now, imagine they were suddenly cut off from their meds. Yeah, there will be some folks to worry about.

For that reason, our step begins in the pharmacy. We aren't going to build a capability to treat the world or run a clinic, but each member of your group who is on medication (of any kind) needs to build their own stockpile. You can do this by re-ordering early if you are on a refill-by-mail plan. Generally, they allow you to refill at 60 to 70 days on these plans for 90-day supply. If you do that for one year, you will have built up quite an extra stockpile. Manage your expiration dates though. You can also ask your doctor for samples on every visit.

In a full-collapse or prolonged WROL situation (civil war, major disaster), your team should pick up any medications they come across and turn them in to your medical team. As usual, I don't advocate looting attacks or anything of the sort, but if you find unsecured and unattended goods, it does no one any good to leave them abandoned.

Medications being scarce is another reason why in TW-03, Defensive Operations, I said that you need to keep medical supplies guarded and secure. There will be addicts looking for any source. Someone under great stress, even a trusted member of your team, may succumb to wanting something to self-medicate. Keep them locked up and guarded, they are valuable and dangerous, just like your weapons.

We aren't going to get into long-term treatment of mental illness or addiction here. The sad truth and harsh reality is that most of these issues are going to "work themselves out" in the first 3 to 6 months of a major WROL situation anyway. It sucks, but that's the truth, and you can't save the whole world.

What we will deal with are short-term stress-related issues that will inevitably come up and how to deal with someone in a short-term crisis to encourage long-term survival.

First and foremost, is an admonition that comes from hard won experience. Any combat zone veteran can tell you a story or two about this warning. You need to establish a policy right off that ANYONE exhibiting any sort of crisis behavior or self-harm ideation will be immediately and completely disarmed. This means guns, knives, ammunition, anything. There is no negotiation to be had here. Make sure that there is no stigma attached to this. Too many times we have failed to do this to protect a guy's ego, and it ended in tragedy, sometimes taking more than one life. It is not up for negotiation.

The next thing is to foster an environment where your people are free to talk to each other about their stress. All the bravado and tough guy stuff needs to go out the window. Seeing death and, God forbid, taking human life (even when warranted) is emotional. You need to let those emotions out. Have an informal mechanism for this, even if it's just a discussion around a dinner table or campfire.

I'm not going to beat anyone over the head with this, because it's not my style, but faith and having a Bible around can go a LONG way in helping. Lt Col Grossman's book "On Combat" can help too. And for my Pagan followers (you ungodly heathens that I love), I acknowledge that whatever faith you have, having its guiding principles on hand in printed form can help. The Hávamál comes to mind, as does the I Ching (Book of Changes).

On that note, having a library among your group is a great way to reduce stress. Reading and writing reduce stress. Collect books as well as supplies.

Prevention also involves having physical outlets for stress. There will be plenty of physical labor, but you also need fun physical things. In Red Dawn, they played football. It can be that simple. Me and my guys are all Tang Soo Do instructors, so martial arts training is a great way to reduce stress. Tai Chi is nothing more than doing martial arts forms in slow motion to stretch and calm the mind. Weight equipment or other fitness gear can help. Just have a plan for fitness and stress reduction.

Sleep Management as First Aid

The best way to prevent stress-related breakdowns among your team is to manage sleep. US military leaders learned this lesson the hard way with increased suicides and declining performance leading to other casualties. People not getting enough sleep perform the same as intoxicated people, with poor decision-making skills and slowed reaction times.

People, regardless of what they tell you, need an average of 7 to 8 hours of sleep per 24-hour period. I worded it that way because there is evidence that you don't need uninterrupted sleep to recover. Some doctors will disagree, but the truth is that we don't know all the science behind sleep. Studies indicate that as long as you aggregate 7 to 8 hours of sleep every 24 hours, you can perform at peak efficiency.

This is important, because we know that we need to maintain security and do all kinds of other tasks. Understand that taking two 4-hour sleep sessions gets you to the same place as 8 hours of uninterrupted sleep. Make sure that everyone is getting enough sleep. Leaders should develop sleep plans because sleep is just as important as every other survival activity.

If you had to run a 48-hour patrol with only 3-4 hours of sleep, take the next 24-hour period to ensure that everyone involved catches up on sleep. Sleep deprivation is cumulative; it can build over several days. You occasionally will need to stop and catch up.

Encourage your people to report when they aren't able to sleep or aren't getting enough sleep. A lot of people will try to keep this to themselves out of fear of letting the team down, but I assure you that if they can't perform or fail miserably due to exhaustion, they will let the team down more.

When someone reports a sleep issue, leaders should put them on light duty and have them rest. If they are having issues falling asleep, diphenhydramine (Benadryl) can help. It's a sleep aid as well as an antihistamine, just be sure not to give too much.

Dealing with Emotional Disturbed Persons (EDP)

Let's be honest, in a WROL situation, there will be a lot of disturbed folks around. One of your SOP's should be to KEEP

ON WALKING when you encounter one. I know, it's hard, but you are trying to survive, not cure the world. You don't have the resources and support structure to handle folks with mental illness or acute neurological stress in most cases. The best thing to do is to give them a wide berth and press on.

That being said, sometimes one will appear at a checkpoint or gate, or you may come across a crime scene (think raiders hitting a farm) and this individual may be the only person able to give you the information you need. Alternatively, a member of your group may display signs of abnormal behavior.

The first tip is to monitor your people for sudden changes in behavior, affect, or mood. Things to look for are:

- Changes in attitude, behavior, or personality.
- Sudden change in daily habits.
- Uncontrolled outbursts of temper.
- Disorganized thinking.
- Distrust & hypersensitivity.
- Hallucinations, fear, and delusions.

If you can intervene before it develops into a crisis, you are far better off.

People in crisis can react violently without logical reason, so safety is paramount. To protect against this, we use the "Contact and Cover" principle. One person will make contact with the subject, while a second moves around to the left or right rear, in order to intervene to protect the contact person should that become necessary. The contact person should have any weapons holstered or slung, or better yet, be unarmed (they can't take away what you don't have). This one thing will calm the disturbed person greatly and the cover person can protect the contact person.

When dealing with emotionally disturbed people:

- Don't lie or deceive – it will destroy trust.
- Let them vent no matter what. They will usually calm down afterwards.
- Don't verbally abuse them, no matter what they say to you.
- Avoid threats – they never work.
- Use the least amount of force necessary if you have to restrain them.
- Remain calm yourself – "The anger of man seldom works…" (James 1:20).

You need to approach from a friendly and helpful posture, rather than one of authority. Understanding goes a long way to calming.

Remember – these folks must be disarmed. If it's a member of your team, that's easy as there is already trust built up. In a WROL situation with someone you don't know, they are not exactly going to be willing to drop their arms. If you have women with you, they are generally better at getting other women and even men to comply. In the case of someone who doesn't know and trust you, showing them that you are unarmed and asking them to at least put their arms on the ground next to them can start you on the process. Then, by movement and talking, you can get them to walk away from their weapons, but don't pick up their arms, it will scare them. Leave them there.

Ask them what has brought them to where they are, and that can help them start thinking logically again. For members of your own team, get them talking about routines and teamwork, and it will usually bring them around.

We aren't actually treating anything here, so let's remember that. We are MANAGING the symptoms by getting them to calm down and get a grip on reality again. As I've said before, we won't have the ability to provide care. For outsiders, calm them, get what information you can, and maybe give them some hope by sending them towards areas that you have heard are more stable. Don't fall for sob stories and let them in to your group. Don't let them follow you. If you have extra, maybe leave them some food, but you can't always be the hero here. A good idea is to ask them what supplies they have. This will again get them to think about survival and making logical thought patterns. It can also show them that they have survival potential.

On this note, if they were armed and you've calmed them, then go ahead and pick up their arms. Explain that you are going to remove the ammunition and drop the firearm further down the road for them. This is for your safety. Don't leave them the firearm at first, they might have other ammunition. Hand their ammunition or magazines to them.

If you encounter someone you just can't calm down, you should then just gather your team and leave. If they follow, you might have to restrain them and leave them somewhere. Be sure not to restrain them to the point that they will be defenseless or die, just enough to delay them from following. Tied to a tree with a length of rope with a tight but workable knot is enough. It's hard but has to be done for security.

116

When it's a member of your own team, it's harder. Do everything you can to encourage talking it out with each other. The power of talking to others with similar experiences cannot be underestimated. You can prevent a lot of these issues by talking and then sharing the good that has gone on. In a world of horrible things, every spot of good should be celebrated.

Suicidal Ideation

Establish right now that everyone on your team must report suicidal comments or actions to leadership or the medical team immediately. There is no room for secrets in this area.

The first person to contact a suicidal member of your team needs to get the victim talking. The longer they talk, the more likely they are to change their mind. Avoid sudden or aggressive movement around a suicidal person. I know, the first thought is to come running to prevent it, but you can help a lot more by calmly walking up and asking them how they are doing.

Keep uninvolved people away to preserve privacy but get another person or two in a position to help you restrain the victim if needed. Do so quietly and slowly. Be patient and understanding while listening. Convince the victim of the good your group is doing and their part in it. Let them see the long-term survival potential.

Don't be afraid to let them know that without them, the risk for the rest of the team goes up. Knowing that others rely on them can help. Don't be above triggering that millennia old honor principle in each of us – it has worked in combat theaters.

Don't worry if it takes hours, a life is at stake. Talk it out. If it's an interpersonal dispute, listen. Then later talk to the other half.

If you've arrived and an attempt has already been made, render whatever first aid you can while preventing them from doing further harm. Secure any weapons and gather any pill containers for your medical team. Ensure that after they've been treated, someone sits down and talks with them to resolve the issue.

Suicide watch is a thing because it works. If you've calmed someone, remind them that they will not be assigned armed duties for at least 48 hours and only after another evaluation. Then, let them know that they will be under supportive observation. There is no secret and no stigma. Each person on the watch must take it seriously. They need to talk with the person but not patronize them. Good natured humor goes a long way to strengthening each other, more so than patronizing. Those on suicide watch should also not be armed.

Anxiety

Anxiety is a general feeling of unease, fear, or apprehension. Naturally, life in a WROL environment can cause anxiety. Find out if the anxiety is causing them to lose sleep or appetite, or if it is impairing their ability to work. With potential anxiety, ALWAYS ask about feelings of self-harm. It's better to ask and risk upsetting someone than to risk someone harming themselves.

Symptoms of anxiety include:

- Skittish; easily startled or distracted.
- Restlessness and hypervigilance.

118

- Rapid, breathless speech (but may also stutter).
- Thoughts of hopelessness and dread (suicide risk).
- Mood is worried and sad.

Treatment involves teaching them relaxation breathing. Combat breathing (inhale for a count of 4, hold for 4, exhale for 4) is a great way to reduce anxiety. Have the patient visualize themselves somewhere relaxing and calm. Ask them what helps to reduce stress and relax and incorporate this into a treatment plan.

Anxiety is a symptom of Acute Stress Disorder. This is anxiety and stress over a traumatic event. It generally presents itself within 4 weeks and resolves itself in another 4 weeks from onset. When it does not resolve, it can develop into Post Traumatic Stress Disorder. Work actively to help people put things in their proper perspective (We are trying to maintain order and survive – it was others who choose the wrong path).

Since you won't have access to many medications, your treatment options are only what was discussed above.

It's important to let an anxiety victim know that they aren't crazy and that this is normal. Keep them on duty but restrict anything with caffeine in it.

Operational Stress/Battle Fatigue

This is a problem that has had many names throughout history. Shell-shocked is the most common, but of course now we have to have technical sounding names.

For those not acclimated to it, being thrown into a combat situation or a complete collapse of society around them is very stressful. This can lead to severe, paralyzing stress. We call that Battle Fatigue.

Symptoms include anxiety, terror, guilt, sadness, depression, hallucination, insomnia, hyper-alertness, erratic actions, panic running, and loss of hope/faith. Ask how long they've felt this way – if longer than a few days, then there is potential for a more serious issue. Ask them if they can fight or do their job as this usually refocuses the patient on the team and their ability to function. As with anxiety, ask about thoughts of self-harm.

Treatment follows the acronym PIES:

P   Proximity – keep them with their teammates for continuity.

I   Immediacy – Start treatment as soon as tactically possible with someone who developed an issue during a crisis.

E   Expectancy – Let them know that they will get better and that this is perfectly normal.

S   Simplicity – Most cases are resolved by the 4 R's:

Rest – Let them get rest. If you have someone trained, Valium (5mg) or Ativan (1-2 mg) in small doses can help.

Reassurance – Let them know it will get better/easier.

Replenishment – Everything looks better after eating and drinking some water, and a shower.

Restoration – Restore their confidence. Give them tasks to do while recovering, which will make them feel less like they are letting everyone down.

The Stress of Dealing with Bodies

Now here is one of the things that no one in preparedness talks about, because it's not cool. You will have to deal with a large number of dead bodies. It's just a fact. Estimates are that after one year without electricity, 90% of Americans will be dead. I'm not convinced of that number myself, but there will be a large number.

All the movies and TV shows show the cool guys slugging it out with the bad guys and afterwards, they move on to the next mission, leaving the dead bad guys to magically disappear. Well, in real life, most of the dead will be innocents, and someone must remove even the bad guys, because if you don't disease will follow quickly.

Most people will quickly be repulsed to see the victims of battle or a natural disaster, but they must still be dealt with. We can't just leave them. There will be grotesque injuries, there will be children and the elderly, traditionally to be protected, among the dead. They must all be recovered and dealt with. Covering bodies early on can make the work a little easier.

First, discuss the morality of the recovery operation with everyone. It is right and proper to respectfully treat the dead, even hostile dead. The safest thing to do from a health perspective is to burn the dead, but most cultures frown on that. What most cultures do accept is burial, even if it is in a mass grave. While the work will be horrific and stressful, the act of putting the dead to rest in the ground is therapeutic in and of itself.

When members begin to show signs of stress, talk it out. Remind them that if it was a family member, they would want someone to do what we are doing. Remind them of the need to bury the bodies to prevent disease or attracting dangerous wildlife. One strategy if someone is really stressed about it is to assign them to the documentation whatever identification you can find, letting them feel as if they might give someone closure later on. Let them see a purpose in the grim work.

When the mass grave is filled, have someone say a few words according to whatever faith they follow. It's OK if more than one faith speaks. The words said are more for your team standing there and we might as well pray for the souls of the dead.

To combat stress, take frequent breaks. Talk to each other and check on each other. It is indeed a grim task, but it must be done.

Ensure that everyone wears gloves and a mask during the operation and have everyone tend to personal hygiene as soon as the task is over.

Recap

This is the level of neurological emergencies that you have the realistic capabilities to deal with. There are many, many other issues, but they are beyond the scope of this manual.

Your medical team will have personnel who are more capable of handling more advanced issues and some of the reference books listed in the appendix can help. They go into further detail than we can here.

We aren't making doctors; we are training the entire team on lifesaving steps.

Training Standard

1. List steps that can be taken to reduce stress.

2. Explain why sleep management matters.

3. Describe how to identify and deal with emotionally disturbed persons.

4. Explain how to handle suicidal ideation.

5. Explain the symptoms of anxiety and how to treat it.

6. Explain Battle Fatigue and how to treat it.

7. Describe the steps to take while disposing of the dead.

Tactical Wisdom

First Aid Manual

Chapter 11

Managing Illnesses

Worship the Lord your God, and his blessing will be on your food and water. I will take away sickness from among you.

Exodus 23:25

We have to admit to ourselves right up front that the average team won't have the resources to provide full medical care and cure illnesses and diseases. However, we will have the ability to manage the symptoms and attempt to prevent illnesses from running rampant throughout our team.

We're not going to everything here, because this isn't that kind of book. The resources listed in the appendix will have more information and you really need to recruit medical professionals into your group. We're talking about managing the symptoms of everyday ailments.

In a world without advanced medical care, sickness and illness are real issues. I can't just run to CVS and pick up some severe cold medicine and go on with my day. Even colds and the flu left unchecked can run through a camp and kill.

Quarantines

I know, this is a touchy subject after COVID. We're going to take the Biblical approach here. In order to prevent illness from running through your whole team, the ill will be expected to self-segregate as much as possible and not expose others.

Obviously, let your medical team make the final decision, but most will just self-report and a take a sick day. You can find work them to do that is solo in nature to protect everyone.

Nausea

Nausea is a symptom of many things. Managing it is hard.

Vomit must be cleaned up as soon and as thoroughly as possible. Exposure to it can infect others and vomit breeds more vomiting.

The following are steps to reduce nausea:

1. Drinking clear and/or ice-cold drinks.
2. Eating light, bland foods (such as saltine crackers or plain bread).
3. Avoiding fried, greasy or sweet foods.
4. Eating slowly and eating smaller, more frequent meals.
5. Not mixing hot and cold foods.
6. Drinking beverages slowly.
7. Avoiding activity after eating

Plain rice is a good food to stop nausea. Cinnamon, ginger, and chamomile teas also are treatments for nausea. Inhaling peppermint and lemon can help.

Reducing Fever

Fevers can be very dangerous, especially high ones in adults. Reducing a fever quickly is always a good thing. While we can take fever reducers now, in a prolonged WROL situation, we might need more homeopathic solutions.

Clinical treatments in the current world are:

1. Take acetaminophen or ibuprofen to help bring the temperature down.
2. Drink plenty of fluids, particularly water.
3. Avoid alcohol, tea and coffee as these drinks can cause slight dehydration.
4. Sponge exposed skin with tepid water.
5. Avoid taking cold baths or showers. Skin reacts to the cold by constricting its blood vessels, which will trap body heat.
6. Make sure you have plenty of rest, including bed rest.

The best home remedies are rest and drinking broth (bone broth is best).

Cough Home Remedies

Managing a cough is rough. Your medical supplies should include a good number of cough drops. These are great for guys on patrols or manning Observation Posts to prevent making noise as well as treating a cough.

Cold and cough medicine is great to stockpile, but if you run out of it, you might need a home remedy.

The following home remedies can help:

1. Honey: a teaspoon or two.
2. Hot drinks
3. Steam
4. Ginger tea: mix with honey
5. Elderberry (either extract or syrup)
6. Menthol (peppermint)

Other, more serious illnesses are beyond the scope of this manual, but more information can be found in the books listed in the resources in the Appendix.

Training Standards

1. List ways to reduce nausea.

2. List ways to reduce fever.

3. List home remedies for a cough.

Tactical Wisdom

First Aid Manual

Chapter 12

Field Sanitation

As part of your equipment have something to dig with, and when you relieve yourself, dig a hole and cover up your excrement.

Deuteronomy 23:13

I bet you didn't know that the Bible had a verse on Field Sanitation. Well, now you do. As long as man has lived in communities, sanitation has been an issue. We learned quickly that our waste handling, food handling, and water sourcing were paramount to survival. Thousands of years later, things haven't changed one bit.

I know, we've covered field sanitation before, but it's so vital that we are going to go over it again, and in more depth. It is 100% a life-or-death matter. It's just not as cool as other things, but I assure you it's far more important.

Imagine the impact on a city of even just 30,000 if the sewer system stopped working. The health implications of 30,000 people needing to relieve themselves multiple times a day in relatively close proximity would lead to multiple pandemics of epic proportion.

Most of the world remains undeveloped. It is our western way of life that is the anomaly in the world. Sure, you can go to Lagos, Johannesburg, Mumbai, or Saigon and find modern conveniences, but drive just 25 miles out of the city and you will find no sewers and no treated water. And people not only survive but thrive in these conditions. So can you, as long as you know how to handle this.

In 2013, 1.77 billion people worldwide used pit latrines (holes in the ground), while another 892 million used "open defecation" or no toilets. With a world population of 8 billion, this means 1 in 4 people. It can be done, as long as it is done right.

One study showed that in 2011, 700,000 school aged children died from infectious diarrhea. This is spread when flies hover around fecal matter, then around our food. It's a leading cause of diarrhea and intestinal worms. We should have a plan to combat this.

A caution for those thinking they can bug in and just manually add water to the toilet tank for flushing: You CAN do that, for a relatively short time. Once the entire sewer system is backed up, you will need to seal off your toilet to prevent raw sewage from erupting into your house. Water in the toilet tank is a temporary solution.

Field sanitation covers preventing infectious things from traveling into your body. In the UK, they developed the "Five F's" of field sanitation. The "Five F's" teach us what to watch for:

Fluids:	Water sources, filtration, and safe storage.
Fingers:	Keeping clean.
Flies:	Controlling pests.
Fields/Food:	Keeping our food and food production clean and safely stored.
Floods:	Having proper drainage to prevent anything from getting contaminated.

A Lesson from the Past

In late 1944, Marines were making their way across Guam and Marine Air Group (MAG) 21 was camped on the Orote Peninsula. After being there a few days, the unit was overcome with dysentery and dengue fever. As we all know from The Oregon Trail, dysentery can kill you.

The Commanding Officer took quick action. He ordered the unit to bury the enemy dead. He instituted unit field hygiene measures and enforced them rigorously. He also had the medical team find a cleaner water source. Once he implemented these measures, dysentery and dengue fever vanished.

Siting Latrines

The first concern we have is where to site our latrines, both for field use and more permanent installations. As a general rule, latrines must be at least 100 feet or 30 meters from any ground water source. If you have some type of communal food storage or prep facility, the latrines should be at least 100 yards/90 meters downwind from it.

The main drawback here is security. It must be outside the living area, even in an overnight camp site. You will need security to go use the latrine.

Whatever type of latrine you build, it should have handwashing facilities just outside it. This can be as simple as a spigot attached to a rainwater collection device. Wipes or hand sanitizer can do in a pinch.

Temporary Latrines

Temporary latrines are for overnight camps or camps of about a one-week duration. For overnight or less, use a cathole latrine and for longer than one day, use a straddle trench. After each use, sprinkle some dirt on top to control flies and odor. Before leaving the site, completely cover the latrine.

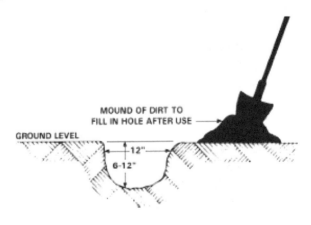

Cat Hole Latrine

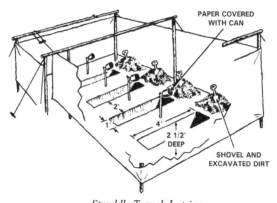

PAPER COVERED
WITH CAN

2'

1'

4'

2 1/2'
DEEP

SHOVEL AND
EXCAVATED DIRT

Straddle Trench Latrine

Remember in TW-02 Fieldcraft and TW-04 Scouting & Patrolling when we talked about carefully evaluating a potential overnight or patrol base site by walking all over the site? This is what we are looking for. You don't want to camp right on top of someone's old latrine.

These are temporary solutions only.

Pit Latrines

We use the Pit Latrine as a more permanent solution. Generally, these can be sustained indefinitely. The outhouse at my parent's cabin has been in use my entire life, and the lives of my grandparents before that. It just takes a little planning.

The same siting rules apply, and you want the bottom of the pit to be above the water table. In other words, if you are digging and hit water, you went too far. The pit should be lined and bottom semi-porous. As the organic material breaks down, it will filter out into the surrounding soil and be further filtered naturally.

That's why it's important to get far enough away from your water source. For lining, you can use a 55-gallon drum with holes poked in the bottom. In some regions, they are fully lined with cement. Lye applied after use can help control odors but it may slow down decomposition.

Here is a plan for a large unit, adjust the size to your needs:

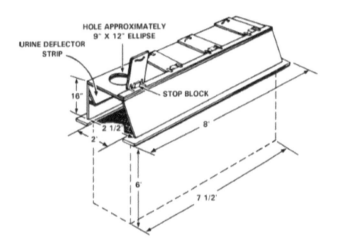

Source: US Marine Corps

If the water table is too high or the ground too hard for digging, you can build upwards and use what is called a "pail latrine". The bad part of the pail latrine is that it must be emptied regularly, and you need somewhere to dispose of the waste safely. Perhaps you can find somewhere else to dig and bury the waste or you can incinerate it, but fuel will be hard to find.

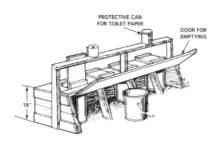

Source: US Marine Corps

Many veterans will remember the burn-out latrines, but we aren't including them here because in our envisioned scenario, we won't have excess gasoline or diesel to burn the waste.

Dealing with Garbage

Even in a survival situation, we will have garbage that will need to be dealt with. Leaving both food packaging, food waste, and organic material around will attract rodents and other pests, which will lead to sickness and illness.

The best option is continuing to use community dumps and landfills. They require no technology and will likely still be operational. This is the best case, but if they aren't, you need to locate a safe location a safe distance away from your living area to bury trash.

When burying trash, bury it deep and cover it with at least 18 inches of hard packed dirt. Let it settle and then cover again. It's a good idea to line the trash pit with some type of barrier (like plastic sheeting) to prevent groundwater contamination.

A better option, despite the screeching of environmentalists, is burning your trash. Place a 55-gallon drum on rocks, with holes punched in the lower 1/3. You can put a grate near the bottom. I recommend having an expanded metal cover to place over the barrel to prevent animals from crawling in. Place the waste in the barrel and burn it. You can then bury the ashes. There are also commercially available burn barrels on the market.

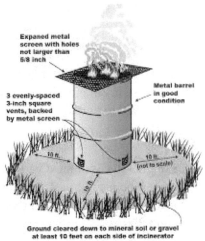

Expaned metal screen with holes not larger than 5/8 inch

Metal barrel in good condition

3 evenly-spaced 3-inch square vents, backed by metal screen

10 ft.

10 ft. (not to scale)

Ground cleared down to mineral soil or gravel at least 10 feet on each side of incinerator

A note about the environmental or health impact of burning trash. Most of the world does this. Once you get past the first few months, there will no longer be new plastics and other materials, so the risk of harm goes down. As far as health risks, don't stand there and take deep breaths during the short time the fire burns. Be smart.

You can also compost organic material. Buy a commercial composting bin or create a pile in your yard. You can combine yard waste (grass clippings, leaves, and twigs) with organic material like food waste. Add about 2 to 3 times as much yard waste as food waste. Regularly turn this over with a shovel or rake (or turn the handle on your composter), and eventually this will turn to fertile soil. I am not an expert, and this is just an overview, but it's another tool for you. There are plenty of books and videos available to learn composting.

Personal Hygiene

In other volumes we covered what needs to go into your personal hygiene kit. In this one, we're just going to hit the high points.

If possible, bathe or shower every day. If you can't, do it at least once a week. On days when you can't shower, use a washcloth or wet wipe on areas that sweat and that air doesn't circulate on like the genitals, arms pits, feet, between thighs, between buttocks, and under the breasts. There are a lot of commercially available field wipes, stock up.

You can find camp showers at any outdoor store. This is essentially a rubberized bag with a nozzle attached. You fill it and hang it in a tree to heat up, then turn it on when you need to shower. They are small in capacity, but they work. You can also build a shower with a drum with the top removed to catch rainwater, and an attached hose and nozzle. Painting it black will allow the sun to heat it. It is preferred however to shower in potable water to reduce the chance of sickness.

You need to clean your feet daily. They are your transport. Wash them and thoroughly dry them out every day. Change socks at least once a day and anytime you cross a wet area. Use foot powder if you have it available. You never know when you're going to need to use your feet and quickly.

One of the reasons why Western military units require short hair is disease prevention. In the 1700-1800s, lice and fleas were a common disease vector among soldiers, and then influenza came. Short hair became a military thing. Use soap/shampoo and water whenever you can to clean your hair. Shave every day if possible. Never share combs or brushes. Check each other for lice occasionally. Lice and their eggs will be close to the scalp.

I don't want to sound like a COVID commercial but wash your hands frequently. Use hand sanitizer or wipes, especially before eating and after using the latrine. Wash as soon as possible after coming into contact with humans you don't know in a WROL situation.

Oral Health

That's right, kids, you still have to brush your teeth. In fact, in a world without ready access to medical and dental care, you need to take even better care of your teeth and gums. Not being able to eat because of cavities and mouth pain will take you off the playing field quickly. Take some basic steps to ensure good oral health.

When brushing, use potable water (in other words, purified water). Use toothpaste whenever possible (or brushing powder). However, don't let that be the reason you don't brush. If you don't have toothpaste, still brush and clean the toothbrush thoroughly after. If you don't have a toothbrush, use a clean twig or even your clean finger.

Brush in a circular pattern and don't forget your gums, tongue, and roof of your mouth when brushing. Brush twice a day whenever possible.

Clothing & Sleeping Gear

Taking care of your sleep system and clothing is just as important. Your clothing is your first line of defense against insects and insect-borne diseases, along with a lot of other issues. Keep it clean and in good repair.

If you don't have a sewing kit and a sleep system repair kit, you need to fix that right away. On that note, I also have a tent repair kit and a pair of tarp repair kits. Keeping your clothing, sleep system, and shelter intact is a great way to prevent illness and injury. Prevention, through good repair, is better than treatment for preventable injuries and sicknesses.

You should wash your clothing at least every 7 days. Wash it in a lake or stream and air dry it in the sun (yes, even in the winter it works). Your underwear and socks need to be dried in the sun, especially. The UV rays from the sun kill bacteria. It's free, and will always be there, even when it's cloudy.

Your sleep system can be washed a little less frequently, but still keep it clean. Air dry your sleep system in the sun. If you can't wash it, still hang it in the sun whenever the situation permits.

If you can't wash your clothes after 7 days, you can crush it up and then shake it out vigorously, and then hang it out in the sun. This will refresh it and drive away any insects or bacteria.

Water Purification

Every water source should be considered contaminated, and all water must be treated. Get into the habit of pre-filtering water as you retrieve it by filtering it through a clean cloth as you fill your containers or as you transfer it from temporary containers to treatment containers. This will remove large particles.

Despite all our technological progress, the best way to treat water remains boiling. Bringing water to rolling boil for one minute will kill the majority of bacteria and organisms.

Using big pump filters isn't feasible in the field. If that's what you plan on using, get several containers that you clearly label as "DIRTY" water containers. Fill those, and then take them to a more secure location away from the water source to run it through your filters into your clean containers.

Remember, water sources will draw humans. You want to spend as little time near them as possible.

I opt for filters that can attach directly to my drinking tube. I have an attachment that allows my drinking tube to be used with a hydration bladder or with US 1-quart or 2-quart canteens. This way, I'm not wasting energy and making noise by getting out my canteens and I can filter as I drink.

The other option is some type of purification tablet. There are several kinds on the market, and they are widely available at outdoor stores. I like them because I just drop them into my canteens and keep moving without stopping to purify. Whichever kind you buy, make sure that you read and understand the directions fully. The 2-step types make the water taste better than one step.

You can buy UV filtration options, but they are suboptimal because they require batteries and power to work.

I also don't recommend bleach, because it's too easy to poison yourself and you won't be able to find bleach. Rely on low to no tech options.

Training Standard

1. List the Five Fs of Sanitation.

2. Explain where to site latrines.

3. Demonstrate digging a cat hole latrine.

4. Describe how to build a staddle trench.

5. Explain what a pit latrine is and how to build one.

6. List options for dealing with trash.

7. List the basic steps of personal hygiene.

8. List the actions to take for basic oral hygiene.

9. Describe how to care for your clothing and sleep system.

    a. Obtain a sewing kit.
    b. Get a tent repair kit.

10. List 3 methods of water purification.

Tactical Wisdom

First Aid Manual

Guest Chapter

The Arctic Nurse

*For their Pizza shalt never be defiled by Pineapple and their
French Fries neither by Gravy – for Poutine is an Abomination.*

Book of Tactical Wisdom 1:1

The Artic Nurse not only knows a thing or two about medicine in
an austere environment, but he also lives it. He serves as a
medical practitioner in the farthest and most remote regions of
Canada, well above the Arctic Circle. He asked if he could
provide some tips based on his experience. As long as his advice
doesn't involve pizza toppings or disgusting appetizers from the
frozen wasteland he calls home, we'll listen.

Here is his advice:

Before You Enter

I'm a rural nurse by trade, so I'm used to playing a little fast and
loose with the rules. I've worked at the literal frontiers of human
habitation, with three years in various communities in Nunavut,
and two more years in northern rural positions. I've worked on

reservations on the west coast, in COVID wards in Yellowknife. This is what I do.

While I am a medical professional, you are not. That said, the usual disclaimers apply, and beyond that, I want to remind you that the odds are you have no idea what you're doing. So, I'll recommend you take a deep breath and discard your supply of acetaminophen suppositories. We're going back to basics here: you keep the blood in, the piss out, and treat basic symptoms with OTC drugs. If you try to use a chest needle, you will kill someone.

Savvy?

On the whole, preventative medicine should be your focus when it comes to the wellbeing of your family- and frankly, yourself. It's a lot easier to fix the problem before you need medicine than when you do. Of course, this means a frank assessment of your health, and your family's. So, we're going to be making ABC cards to hand over to medical professionals that may end up treating you or your family.

I break it down into three rough categories: Allergies, Basics, Conditions. The ABCs are a simplified version of admission questions at your typical rural/outpost care center. You walk in the door and tell us your problem. We ask you for those three pieces of information while we get you a puke bucket or make the leaking stop. Having them on a card for everyone in your family group, ready to go is also essential - if I am rendering aid, and you can't speak, I'm going to make educated guesses trying to save your life. For example, if you catch pneumonia and are delirious due to your fever, you probably can't tell me you're allergic to sulfa medications. I give you the antibiotics I have on hand, and poof, your day just got a lot worse.

The first thing you should be concerned about is allergies. If you or your family have allergies, you NEED Medic Alert bracelets. You also need EpiPens, if it's an anaphylactic reaction- at least three per allergic person. Fun fact- EpiPens are designed to get you to a medical facility, and in 80% of cases, a medical professional (i.e., me) administers the second dose, along with a healthy dose of IV/IM Benadryl. Now, you may ask "Why, Sasha, do we need three?" Well, three gives you 45 minutes to get to advanced medical care if symptoms don't subside. Three gives you 30 minutes if they're expired (not recommended practice, but in extremis - it's better than the alternative.)

Basics are simple things, like medical history. Write on an index card everyone's name, birth date, history of things like surgeries, pregnancies, injuries, allergies and existing conditions. This will help someone trying to help you determine what's going on if existing medical records can't be accessed.

Conditions are existing issues that you or your loved one has, from your kid's diabetes to your dad's high blood pressure, to your husband's asthma. Add them to the cards, as well as what prescribed medications they have including times and dosages. Also, if you're taking any regular, scheduled medications, such as heart pills in the morning, jot that down too.

Habits dictate your health. Whether that's going for a run first thing in the morning, to that Baconator you grab on the way home because you're just beat after work, it all profoundly affects your day-to-day health. When's the last time you had your yearly physical? Ladies, a pap smear? Had a cleaning or a dentist's appointment? It'd suck to die of a tooth abscess now, wouldn't it? Another habit you need to change is your diet. No more takeout- I know you're tired, I know it tastes good, but hear me out: maybe the reason you're tired all the time is your diet. Fast food isn't nutritional. It's designed to make you not hungry anymore, and save you time, that's it. It's unhealthy at best. Same thing with nice takeout - you order too much, overeat, oversleep. You feel tired. You put garbage into your body, and you get garbage out. That said, I'm not a nutritionist - and I'm not your doctor. For me, one thing that's worked to increase my energy, combat my literally crippling depression and keep my energy up has been upping the red meat in my diet. A steak or sausage breakfast goes a long way. Smoking my own meat is not only relaxing but saves me money and gives me a healthy product.

I'm not going to give you the rote 'get fit and survive' lecture. You're going to get it a lot, with people telling you to ruck march and lift three times your bodyweight. But I want you to do a dedicated workout at least twice a week and do one physical activity on the weekend. Heck, ride your bike to work, get your groceries on foot, just get fit. I know you're tired, I know you're hurting inside and out, but like getting sutured, you got to hurt to heal. You'll get more energy soon enough, you'll feel better.

The Water Trap:

Okay, so you may not have a balcony, but you should have windows. Removing the panes and putting up a tarp will conceal you and gives you the opportunity to build a simple water trap, to funnel rain or snow into a container like a cooking pot (seriously, don't use a bucket - the chances of cross contamination with poop and chemicals is too high), for purification.

It's simple stuff- measure the window. Get a tarp folded and pinned to the window frame at roughly 1.5 times the length of said window. Pin the tarp to the window frame so it covers your window, but allows you to pull up the bottom corners for observing the neighborhood.

When it rains, remove the center pinning, open the window, put a broom handle in the center. It should provide you with a 45-degree triangle to funnel water into your pot to boil and purify.

On Pooping:

Okay, so at some point, you're going to have to take a dump while the toilet no longer works. The first thing you need to know is that you can, in fact, flush a toilet without running water, and it's a good way to get rid of 'grey water', e.g., the stuff you've used to clean yourself and dishes. Just pour that into your toilet tank, and you can probably get a flush in. Another alternative is...well, just urinating in the toilet tank. Unpleasant, but so is piling up turds that can't be flushed. After that...well, you have one option. It goes out a window or off the balcony. That means exposure, briefly - but after a while, it will become something of an obstacle. Anyone scavenging will be looking for easier prey than 'cross poop pile, then climb 17 flights of stairs to try and break into a floor, then an apartment door'.

This may not work, however. You could have too little water, there may be a jam down the line, the system may be full. In a house or semidetached setting, the chances of this are negligible, but possible - which is why you need to figure out the location of your nearest storm drain. If it's right outside your house, it's easy enough to pour in quickly.

"But Sasha," you ask, "Why not just dig a pit in my backyard?"

Well, first of all, you'll be exposed for however long that may take. It's noisy, exhausting, and some dude digging in his backyard will be noticed. Then, once you pour all of it in, you need to cover it up. It's a tradeoff - less exposure, more efficiency. An open latrine in your backyard is a good indication of someone living there, and therefore a target. It's also a bit of a daunting barrier once someone gets over or through your fence. It covers the smell of cooking, too.

This is another reason to get as high up off the ground floor of an apartment. Your solution is a lot less elegant - but it will cover the smell of cooking and present something of a barrier to entry.

Your effluent drops will form what is effectively a 'fecal moat'. And, as they say, better out than in. You'll be somewhat distant there, to boot.

Laxatives

Listen, many of you have been in the field eating MRE's before. We all know we get plugged up when we're eating low quality food, sweating and not getting enough water. But strangely, even some basic stuff like Metamucil packets get left behind when you're in the field. In an extended emergency, being full of feces is...not good. Whether it's autonomic dysreflexia (a potentially fatal condition, generally caused by constipation or drug use), gut hits resulting in fecal contamination of the abdominal cavity, or just plain old bowel perforation, it's unpleasant. The rule of thumb is less than three bowel movements a week is bad. More than three days between bowel movements is also a no-no.

At the end of the day, it would just be embarrassing to die of constipation, so pick up that generic fiber-based laxative and use it to flavor your water.

De Rei Mental Health

Yeah, it's going to be a real issue. Whether or not it's you after zeroing someone for the first time, the losses of people close to you, or just...the grind of it all, you need to understand that people will be broken. A routine assessment is usually a short form Mental Health Status exam.

Start with the three D's: Dress, deportment, demeanor. Is the person you are concerned about dressed for the weather, are their clothes clean, are they slumped over or standing tall? Are they carrying themselves appropriately, relaxed or on guard? Are they wearing clothes appropriate to the season and weather? Are they anxious, pacing, angry? Do they look older than they actually are (a sign of substance abuse or extended periods of high stress)? You can do all this as they come in the door, and it can indicate a problem.

After that, we move on to the three A's: Affect, action, and abuse. Do they smell like alcohol? When speaking to you, are they animated, standing, yelling, waving their arms. Is their affect flat when it should be animated or sad? This is where you start to look at both the content of their speech and their mannerisms seriously.

If they aren't right, or they aren't within norms, it might be time to hide the liquor, watch them a little more closely, and sit and talk with them. Currently, PTSD treatment post combat leans towards sitting with people you know and talking it out. Isolating people, making them not feel like part of the team, has led to disastrous consequences.

Pharmacology 101

The first thing you need to know about pharmacology is…know your patient. Firstly, are they allergic to what you're going to give them? Second, do they have any conditions that preclude them taking whatever medication you're about to give them? Thirdly, do you understand the medicine you're about to give them, and is it appropriate? Do they consent to taking the medication? Is the route you're giving them appropriate? Are you giving an infant a pill roughly the width of your wrist? Are you cramming suppositories into a patient perfectly capable of eating?

In all seriousness, what I do recommend is having about 500ml of both Benadryl and Tylenol liquid, on hand. More is better, of course - particularly of the Tylenol.

Now, you may ask, "But, I am grown adult man/woman/rhinoceros, Sasha. Why do I need liquid instead of pills?"

Well, I'm glad you asked. Beyond a noise component while moving, ever tried to give a six-month-old a crushed Tylenol in jam? Yeah, it's pure nightmare fuel. And while you personally may not have an infant, what about your friend's kids? What about your mother or father, or grandparents? What about you, if someone clocks you in the face with a rifle butt or ball peen hammer? Liquid is more efficient in terms of carrying capacity, delivery route, and overall, in terms of delivery. It doesn't involve butt stuff, veins, or chewing. It also helps with pediatric dosing, as liquid doses of, say, Tylenol for fever control are easier to calculate and deliver than 500mg Extra Strength Back Relief Tylenol.

The Cabinet

You've suffered enough, I suppose, for a cabinet list. I've designed this specifically for the lay person. It's a list of the ideal pharmacy to keep at home. Yes, I realize it's extensive, and bulky, but the odds of you getting sick are high. If one member of your household gets sick, odds are more will too. You can't be splitting aspirin pills into quarters with a Ka-Bar to ration them because you've been dipping into your only bottle every time your back hurts. This will be, of course, location dependent - both in terms of supplies and availability. For instance, I have a rather robust personal pharmacy because I can purchase Robaxacet C and Tylenol Ones over the counter here in Canada. Likewise

151

generic formulations are important. Now, something not everyone does, but it's critical:

Get drug cards for everything in your cabinet. Understand the contraindications and proper uses for each one. Understand interactions with the medications you're already taking, and the maximum doses for each one.

MUH KNEES HURT AND I HAVE A FEVER

- ASA, 81mg, chewable pill x 50 (300 if it is a routine medication for someone in your household)
- ASA, 325mg pills , two large bottles
- Acetaminophen liquid, 1L
- Acetaminophen tablets, 500mg, 500
- Robaxisal- 75 tablets, any formulation. Primarily for back pain.
- Ibuprofen 325mg, 500 tablets

MUH SKIN ITCHES AND I CAN'T STOP SNEEZING

- Benadryl Liquid, 300ml
- Benadryl tablets, 50 mg, 150 (Off label use: sleep aid)
- Polysporin Antibiotic Eye Drop, 5 bottles (Can be used for ears as well)
- Calomine Lotion, 500ml
- Day and Nyquil, 500ml each
- Mupirocin, 3x tube (topical cream for infections)
- Polysporin Antibiotic, 3x tube (more is always better)

MUH TUMMY HURT

- Imodium, both liquid and pills, ideally 50 doses of each
- Diovol, 100 tabs
- Gravol 50 tabs, two bottles liquid (Off label use: sleep aid)
- Lactulose, 500ml
- Fiber-Based Laxative, 1 lb, ideally in pre-measured sachets.

Learning Points:

1. Assess yourself and everyone in your household for critical healthcare issues and norms.
2. Assemble allergy, medication, and condition cards for your family, and place copies in other preparations you currently have.
3. Begin locating, pricing and assembling your home pharmacy.

Tactical Wisdom

First Aid Manual

Warrior Study

Luke the Evangelist

Our dear friend Luke, the doctor, and Demas send greetings.

Colossians 4:14

Saint Luke was a physician and a historian. Luke is considered one of the Four Evangelists, represented with Christ in the Jerusalem Cross that we use as a logo. He is generally considered to be the author of both the Book of Luke and the Book of Acts. The styles of both books are similar and use a dry wit that Luke was known for.

What most don't consider, though, is that Luke played a significant role as a spy and a resistance leader, helping Saint Paul smuggle his letters out of prison and delivering them to a network of messengers and safe houses.

Early life in The Way, as the Church was called, was a life of defiance. The Roman Empire had outlawed it, and both the government and religious authorities were hunting them down. Most famously, Paul was leading that hunt before Jesus touched his life and turned him around. The early Church had to meet in secret and keep changing meeting locations, for fear of government raids and infiltration. Sound familiar?

We know that Luke was born between 1 AD and 16 AD in Antioch, Syria. Now, that's not Syria of today, it would be closer to Antakya, Turkey (Antakya is Turkish for Antioch). It is believed that he was hung or crucified from an olive tree at the age of 84 in Thebes. Luke is the only author in the New Testament who was not a Jew.

While Luke never claims to have been an eyewitness to the acts of Jesus, it is believed that he may have been one of the 70 Disciples sent out by Christ. A text called "On the Seventy Apostles of Christ", both Mark and Luke are listed as going on the mission. The text stated that Luke was crucified on an olive tree and Mark was burned to death, which both match other accounts. Ironically, Stephen, the First Martyr, was also one of the Seventy.

We know that Luke traveled with Paul, because throughout Acts, Luke uses "we" when describing the events, and Paul repeatedly reports in his letters that Luke is with him, even saying in 2 Timothy 4:11, "Only Luke is with me". In our context, Luke and Paul were a tactical buddy pair.

Life in the early Church was tough. The authorities, both governmental and religious, were hunting them down. Paul was arrested several times, mostly for inciting insurrection despite not having incited any insurrections (again, sound familiar?).

It was during his long imprisonment in Rome that Luke stayed by his side. It is believed that the Romans allowed Luke to visit because Luke was a physician and claimed to be Paul's doctor.

Here's the first piece of Tactical Wisdom: Cover for action. Luke knew that Paul needed no doctor, but that Paul needed to encourage the Church not to give up. We see them producing the Epistles, which would now compare to a resistance newsletter. They were full of encouragement, telling the Church to stay in the fight, stay the course, and commit to their principles. Luke smuggled them out of the prison and to the network of messengers (intelligence network) of the early church.

For our purposes, we should always have cover for action. For example, having an Amateur Radio or GMRS license is cover for a group of guys with radios. Another example is buying a small game hunting license, which in most states gives you a valid reason to be transporting a "truck gun". Knowing what's in season and possessing a valid hunting license is cover for action. In many states, carrying a "hunting knife" or large fixed blade, is legal with a hunting license - cover for action.

Since many of Paul's letters were in response to letters he received from the churches, we can assume that Luke smuggled them into the prison as well. Otherwise, Paul couldn't have written his Epistles. Ensure that your network communicates in both directions.

The early church also had a safe house network. Throughout both Paul's letters and Luke's books, we see them reference staying and meeting in the homes of other church members. They stayed in safe houses because they were being hunted. There's a lesson in there.

Another thing that turns out to be Tactical Wisdom smuggled out of the prison by Luke was Paul's warnings against "false teachers", or INFORMANTS. Paul warned about several false teachers trying to infiltrate the early church and either help the State destroy them or help the Jewish authorities bring the churches back into their folds. Most often, a church member would send a letter to Paul asking his opinion about the teachings of these infiltrators and Paul would reply not to trust them but trust the teaching Paul had given them and the Gospel. Essentially, the churches were asking Paul through Luke to conduct a background check and vetting.

Luke and Paul were doing something we should all be doing: Vetting members of our groups and any new people trying to come in. Make sure that they are who they say they are and that their values and ideals match those of your group. You don't want to let folks in who will cause drama, or worse. Also, letting in folks of questionable moral fiber would lead to issues.

Luke was well-known as a historian. He vowed to Paul to write his second book, Acts, as a chronicle detailing Paul's work. That's our next lesson. I've long said that you need a way to document what happens in a WROL situation because things will eventually change and you might need a record of what happened, day by day.

Writing out things is also therapeutic, which ties in with the purpose of this book. As events that trouble us occur, writing down what happened and our thoughts about it is a way to handle the stress. Having some type of notebook and pen is a good start.

Having solid documentation of events can also help you should order be partially or fully restored. When old Mrs. Jenkins tells the Sheriff that her son Leroy was last seen near your location, documenting the issues you had with the Leroy Jenkins crew that led to his untimely demise can protect you.

The most important healing work that Luke performed throughout his days though, was that of being a solid companion to Paul. Paul pointed out frequently that Luke was with him and reassuring him. Remaining steadfast and being a great teammate is the best way we can guard each other's mental health, just as Luke did for Paul. Near the end of his life, Paul wrote that Luke was the only person with him.

Only Luke is with me...

2 Timothy 4:11a

We need to be there for each other just as Luke was for Paul, even to the end. That's what true love amongst brothers looks like. I know it's not from Luke, but Luke illustrated this concept perfectly:

Greater love has no one than this: to lay down one's life for one's friends.

John 15:13

Luke was a great friend, a good physician, and an even better resistance leader.

Tactical Wisdom

First Aid Manual

Appendix

Resources

As I said, this is not a complete resource. Following is a list of books I recommend having in your library.

1. _Auerbach's Wilderness Medicine_, 2-Volume Set by Paul S. Auerbach

2. _Wilderness Medicine_ by M.D. William W Forgey

3. _Wilderness & Travel Medicine: A Comprehensive Guide_ by Eric Weiss

4. _NOLS Wilderness Medicine_ by Tod Schimelpfenig

5. _Where There Is No Doctor_ by David Werner

6. _Where There Is No Dentist_ by Murray Dickson

7. _The Survival Medicine Handbook_ by Joseph Alton & Amy Alton

8. _EMS Field Guide_ by Jon Tardiff

Made in United States
Troutdale, OR
11/17/2024

24861729R00096